THAT
One
Small
Voice

LESSONS AND ACTIONS FROM A
SEXUAL ABUSE SURVIVOR

THAT
One
Small
Voice

LESSONS AND ACTIONS FROM A
SEXUAL ABUSE SURVIVOR

Bridget Goodwin

I HAVE A VOICE PRESS

ISBN: 979-8-99246777-0-3 (E-Book)
ISBN: 979-8-9924677-1-0 (Paperback)
ISBN: 979-8-9924677-2-7 (Hardcover)

Library of Congress Control Number: 2025927696

Disclaimer: This book contains sensitive subject matter related to sexual abuse and trauma. The author has changed names and certain identifying details to protect the privacy of individuals mentioned in this work.

While the experiences shared in this book are based on real events, any references to historical events, real people, or real places have been used with permission or identifying details have been changed. Names, characters, and places may be products of the author's recollection or have been altered to protect individual privacy.

Cover design and book design by Holly Ostrout.
Cover image: "Bird flying to freedom" by photoschmidt from Getty Images. Licensed through Canva Pro.

First edition 2025.

I Have a Voice Press
Kings Mountain, NC
www.ihaveavoice.love

DEDICATION

To the pioneers of faith who have forged a path for my healing and forgiveness.

To the "one," this is for you.

To the love of my life, Johnny, for letting me fly.

CONTENTS

DISCLAIMER

Author's Note: This is my testimony—my truth as I lived it and as it was shared with me by other victims. Abuse is ugly. There is no way to dress it up, to make it sound beautiful or better. I will not sanitize what happened to protect anyone's comfort, because silence protects perpetrators, not survivors.

The events in this book describe sexual abuse that occurred when I was 13 years old. Names have been changed to protect the innocent. Places have been generalized. The abusers are dead. What you will read is the truth of what happened to me from my viewpoint and what was told to me by other victims who trusted me with their stories.

Content Warning: This book contains descriptions of childhood sexual abuse, trauma, and related topics that may be triggering or disturbing to some readers. Reader discretion is strongly advised. This material may be particularly difficult for:

- Survivors of sexual abuse or assault
- Individuals currently experiencing trauma or PTSD
- Minors (parental guidance recommended for readers under 18)

If you are a survivor, please prioritize your mental and emotional well-being. You may wish to read this book with the support of a therapist or trusted friend.

Important Legal and Medical Disclaimer: This book is not a substitute for professional medical, psychological, or legal advice. While I share lessons and actions that have guided my healing journey, every person's experience with trauma is unique. What worked for me may not be appropriate for your situation.

If you are experiencing suicidal thoughts, are in immediate danger, or are in crisis, please contact emergency services (911) or:

- National Suicide Prevention Lifeline: 988 or 1-800-273-8255
- Crisis Text Line: Text HOME to 741741
- RAINN National Sexual Assault Hotline: 1-800-656-HOPE (4673)

The information in this book is based on my personal experience, research, and ministry work. It is intended for educational and inspirational purposes only. I am not a licensed therapist, counselor, psychologist, or medical professional.

You are strongly encouraged to:

- Seek qualified professional help from licensed therapists, counselors, or medical professionals who specialize in trauma

- Consult with appropriate legal professionals if you are considering reporting abuse

- Work with your healthcare provider before making any decisions about your mental or physical health

Limitation of Liability: The author and publisher shall have no liability or responsibility to any person or entity regarding any loss or damage incurred, or alleged to have been incurred, directly or indirectly, by the information contained in this book. By reading this book, you acknowledge that you are solely responsible for your own choices and decisions regarding your healing journey.

Ministry Disclaimer: References to "I Have a Voice" ministry, workshops, healing circles, and related gatherings are descriptions of faith-based peer support and community resources. These are not clinical therapy sessions and do not replace professional mental health treatment. While our ministry collaborates with licensed therapists and counselors in some settings, the ministry itself does not provide licensed therapeutic services.

Copyright and Permissions: All rights reserved. No part of this book may be reproduced, distributed, or transmitted in any form or by any means without prior written permission of the author, except for brief quotations in reviews and certain other noncommercial uses permitted by copyright law.

The stories shared by other victims are used with permission and have been anonymized to protect their identities.

Religious Content: This book contains Christian faith-based content and biblical references that reflect my personal beliefs and my journey of healing through faith. I respect that readers may come from different faith traditions or no faith tradition. Take what resonates with your own spiritual journey and leave what does not serve you.

With love and hope for your healing journey,

—Bridget

"For freedom Christ has set us free; stand firm therefore, and do not submit again to a yoke of slavery." — Galatians 5:1 (ESV)

PRAISE FOR
That One Small Voice

"With courage and candor, Bridget Goodwin recounts the harrowing story of abuse at the hands of a trusted pastor. Combining personal testimony, scientific research, animated poetry and probing questions, That One Small Voice invites readers to experience the hope and healing that Jesus can bring."

—Pastor Stuart Noell, New Covenant Church, Mount Holly, NC

"I witnessed the moment Bridget first shared her story, and the silence in the room at New Life Fellowship was not from disbelief, but from the profound awe of seeing a victim claim her victory. Her book One Small Voice is more than a memoir; it is an incredible testament to the power of courage and the catalyst that inspires us all to speak up. This book will not only move you, it will mobilize you."

—Pastor Rob Massie, New Life Fellowship, White House, TN

"As Bridget slowly and carefully began to share her story, I was and still am struck by the lack of anger and animosity. Our conversations were always centered around how her story could help others dealing with injustice, abuse, or various potentially debilitating hurts. Her story is one of restoration and not retribution. It has been an honor to encourage her to help lead others from the wells of bitterness to the fountain of living waters.'

—Anthony Wilkinson

"I've been amazed & inspired by the fact that, in spite of all Bridget has been through, she STILL loves God. She is a true friend, a true servant of the Lord."

—Judy Wilkinson

"That One Small Voice is more than a book—it's a sacred invitation to healing, restoration, and the reclaiming of identity for survivors of sexual abuse and church trauma. Written by my friend Bridget, a woman whose voice was once silenced by fear and pain, this book is a bold declaration that forgiveness belongs to the abused—not the abuser—and that freedom is found in the arms of a loving Father.

"With biblical truth, raw honesty, and spiritual insight, Bridget offers readers a path toward wholeness. Her story is not just told—it's lived. I had the honor of walking beside her through some of the darkest valleys and witnessing the moment God met her in a run-down hotel, washing away the filthy rags of shame and sorrow. In those sacred minutes, Bridget was transformed. She glowed with the light of Jesus, radiating peace and hope—the very glimmers she now shares in her workshops.

"This book is for every survivor who longs to be seen, heard, and healed. It's for the friends and family who have carried the weight of silence alongside them. That One Small Voice reminds us that God's love is relentless, His grace is abundant, and His healing is real. Bridget's voice may have once been small, but now it echoes with power, purpose, and the promise of redemption. I am so proud of my sister, my friend."

—Christina Mercer

1 If I speak in the tongues of men or of angels, but do not have love, I am only a resounding gong or a clanging cymbal. **2** If I have the gift of prophecy and can fathom all mysteries and all knowledge, and if I have a faith that can move mountains, but do not have love, I am nothing. **3** If I give all I possess to the poor and give over my body to hardship that I may boast, but do not have love, I gain nothing.

4 Love is patient, love is kind. It does not envy, it does not boast, it is not proud. **5** It does not dishonor others, it is not self-seeking, it is not easily angered, it keeps no record of wrongs. **6** Love does not delight in evil but rejoices with the truth. **7** It always protects, always trusts, always hopes, always perseveres.

8 Love never fails. But where there are prophecies, they will cease; where there are tongues, they will be stilled; where there is knowledge, it will pass away. **9** For we know in part and we prophesy in part, **10** but when completeness comes, what is in part disappears. **11** When I was a child, I talked like a child, I thought like a child, I reasoned like a child. When I became a man, I put the ways of childhood behind me. **12** For now we see only a reflection as in a mirror; then we shall see face to face. Now I know in part; then I shall know fully, even as I am fully known.

13 And now these three remain: faith, hope and love. But the greatest of these is love.

(1 Corinthians 13, NIV)

INTRODUCTION

For forty years, I thought I understood these verses about love. I had memorized them, heard them at countless weddings, even lived by them—or so I believed. But I was living with a distorted reflection, seeing love through a mirror that had been cracked and twisted by those who should have protected me.

When someone takes God's beautiful words about love and uses them as chains to bind you, when they speak of protection while harming you, when they twist kindness into control—the very meaning of love becomes clouded. You may know this confusion intimately. Perhaps love has been used as a weapon against you. Perhaps you've wondered if genuine love even exists.

I want you to know it does.

Through my journey from a silenced thirteen-year-old to a woman who now walks alongside other survivors, I've discovered that real love—the love described in these sacred verses—always sets free rather than imprisons. Real love protects the vulnerable rather than exploiting them. Real love "rejoices with the truth" rather than demanding silence.

This book is my gentle hand extended to you, offering to walk with you on a path I've traveled myself. You'll discover not only how to recognize love's counterfeit voices, but how to reclaim love's true voice within yourself. More importantly, you'll learn to hear your own voice again— perhaps for the first time.

Your Journey to Freedom

Through walking alongside other survivors in healing and my own long path to wholeness, I've learned that healing happens in gentle stages. In these pages, you'll discover the same five steps that have brought hope to many who thought their voices were lost forever:

- **Step 1: Breaking the Silence** – Finding the courage to speak your truth, even when your voice shakes

- **Step 2: Recognizing the Patterns** – Understanding how manipulation works, so it can never again work on you

- **Step 3: Reclaiming Your Identity** – Separating who you truly are from what was done to you

- **Step 4: Building Your Community** – Discovering safe relationships where your voice is cherished

- **Step 5: Finding Your Purpose** – Using your healing to create hope for others

This five-step framework has emerged from research and from witnessing transformations in my workshops, conferences and summits as I've walked alongside survivors. My ministry, "I Have a Voice" was founded to give survivors safe spaces to share their stories and break their silence.

In our retreats and healing circles, we work with licensed therapists and counselors who understand trauma's unique challenges. Together, we explore how to rewire your brain and speak truth in your life. You are not what was done to you. You can discover who you truly are, and we'll give you tools to help you daily reclaim yourself and your purpose.

Building your community is the strength of our gatherings. You are not alone. In this safe space, you belong, and it's ok to be yourself. You don't need to hide. We understand your hurt and shame because we've been there too. We share tears when you share your pain, but we laugh and rejoice when you experience breakthrough and find the bravery to speak. You learn that you matter, your voice matters, and your story deserves to be told.

Finding your purpose gives you a commission—you are now equipped to help others find their voice and step into their healing. You learn how to listen and support others. You use what the enemy meant for evil for good. Remember, you have experienced this, and you have witnessed your healing. You know that it can be done. You can be healed. You can find love. You can forgive and find joy in every moment of life because you have chosen to do so. And you will never allow this to happen to anyone else again.

This is what I have witnessed in this healing atmosphere:

- Communities of survivors finding strength in shared experiences
- Guided practice and materials to work through each healing step together
- Licensed therapists and counselors available for private individual support
- Ongoing support and community as survivors implement these practices in their daily lives

Each chapter of my story reveals these steps unfolding—not in perfect order, because healing rarely follows a straight line—but in the beautiful, sometimes messy way that real transformation happens.

Many of the stories throughout this book come from survivors who generously shared their breakthroughs. Their courage inspires me, and their visible transformations confirm that healing isn't just possible—its real. I believe that Jesus has the answers. When you put Him in the equation with surrounded support, and prayer, *"with God all things are possible."* (Matthew 19:26)

A Promise of Hope

I cannot promise that reading my story will be easy. There are chapters ahead that may stir memories you've kept carefully buried. But I can promise you this: if you've survived what brought you to this book, you have the strength to reclaim your voice. I can promise that the same love described in these verses—patient, kind, protecting, persevering—is waiting to enfold you not as a chain, but as wings.

Your cage door may have been locked for years, even decades. But love—real love—always carries the key.

If you're ready to discover that key, if you're ready to hear your own voice singing again, turn the page. I'll be walking beside you every step of the way.

Let me show you how I found my voice. More importantly, let me show you how you can find yours.

CHAPTER 1
Breaking the Silence

"May I fill my speech with love, hope, and freedom. Love holds us together, hope gives us bravery, and freedom cannot be caged."
— Bridget Goodwin

†

Every time I share my story of sexual abuse within the church, another survivor finds the courage to speak. Every time I guide someone through healing in my workshops, I witness the miracle of a voice reclaimed. Through walking alongside other survivors, I've learned that each person's journey toward finding their voice is both deeply personal and surprisingly universal. So, I write to help you find your voice, too.

I've guided survivors through this same transformational process. This proven five-step journey will transform your life as it's transformed my life.

For forty years, I kept a secret that nearly destroyed me. Now I'm breaking my silence—not for vengeance, but so that others can be free.

In the pages that follow, I'll guide you through the same five-step healing journey that developed through my transformed life and the lives of my workshop participants:

1. Breaking the silence that protects abusers

2. Recognizing the manipulative patterns common in church settings

3. Reclaiming your authentic voice and spiritual identity

4. Building a community of support and healing

5. Finding purpose in your pain by helping others

This five-step process forms the foundation of our transformational healing, where survivors find their voices in a safe, supportive community.

This isn't just another story of trauma—it's a practical roadmap to healing specifically designed for those who've experienced abuse within religious communities. When the place that should've been your sanctuary becomes your prison, the betrayal cuts deeper than other forms of abuse. You've lost not just your safety, but potentially your faith community and spiritual foundation. I'll show you how to find freedom without abandoning faith.

You may wonder, "Why now?" I asked my Christian psychiatrist the same question. He told me I could either blame him, my psychiatrist, or tell you, my audience, that I was finally brave enough. I choose the latter. Initially I argued and dismissed the idea of sharing my story. Dr. B. told me I couldn't heal unless I released it, and told my story.

We've Witnessed True Healing

What I've learned through my healing work is that recovery isn't just possible—it's predictable when you have the right roadmap and support. In my healing workshops, I've witnessed transformations that confirm healing is possible at any age.

All names in this book have been changed to protect survivors.

Dinah suffered sexual abuse in the woods as a tiny child, remained silent for decades, then found her voice and shared her experience with us in the safe environment of the workshop. She also experienced forgiveness at a later workshop through our guided process.

Michael carried the secret of abuse by a trusted stepfather for fifty-five years before attending one of my weekend retreats. Many heard his testimony. He unlocked his voice as he stepped out in bravery.

Amber, around eighty, confided in me, whispering about a gut-wrenching dread and darkness stemming from her closely guarded secrets. Her own abuse and others. After seven decades of silence, she finally shared her story with a licensed therapist at my workshop. She could step out of her darkness of isolation and learn to walk in the light of peace. It was clear she was healing. Her face glowed like the sun. She looked so youthful. God had rolled away the darkness.

Jessy thanked me for my workshop and sharing that it was okay to go to a licensed therapist or psychiatrist. She felt like she had permission to start her own therapy. She's now seeing someone and progressing through her own healing journey.

These stories could be yours too. Healing isn't just possible—it's your birthright. These breakthroughs happen regularly in our supportive community, where survivors practice these techniques in a safe, guided environment.

It was difficult when I first shared my story. This won't be different. Writing my story has been very challenging — recalling and reliving my trauma. To be transparent with you,

I've had to take breaks from the writing. The emotional stirrings in my soul were intense — the reliving of memories, the dread, the darkness, the trauma being exposed.

Because of you, I carry on, pen in hand. I want to be that still, small voice: a voice of warning, a voice of rescue, of hope, and healing. A bright torch shining in your cave of darkness that's imprisoned you in its locked cage.

What you can do now: Take a deep breath. Find a quiet space where you feel safe to read this book. Remember, you can set it down and return when you're ready. Your healing journey deserves patience and gentleness.

The Journey of Healing Your Voice Begins Today

My cage felt normal. It was my home. How tragic this was. You may even try to make yourself comfortable in the cage, just trying to cope. Your cage feels "normal."

This isn't normal!

Something has ensnared you.

Has this abuse silenced you? Abuse silences and thrives in darkness. Silence becomes the substitute for being heard and understood. An abuser takes your voice away. It controls you; it cages you. One bar at a time, locking you in.

Imagine losing it for years, your voice distorted, not even a whisper anymore. Maybe this is you. Find a trusted source to speak to. Let the healing begin as you tell your story.

"An untold story never heals." — Mary DeMuth

Through my work with survivors, I've learned that the road to justice is challenging but navigable with the right support. My voice isn't one of revenge. It's not uncommon for survivors of sexual abuse to be questioned, doubted, and revictimized by others, both in and out of their communities, who don't want to believe that happened to them could really happen to people they know and love. But these things do happen and not just to "other people".

I'd like to share with you that I believe you. I'm sorry you've suffered this travesty.

What you can do now: Speak one truth aloud—even if only to yourself in a mirror. Notice how it feels to give voice to your truth, even in this small way.

Recognizing Manipulation in the Church

Have you found that the hole in your heart has become filled with a warped sense of love?

It isn't normal if you're afraid of your relationships with others. You deserve to be treasured and unharmed. Mistreatment twists love when you feel you deserve it. Let me reassure you that you've done nothing to deserve this ensnaring love.

These lies are bars in your cage. I call this a playlist of untruths that came from my abuser:

"Can I trust you?"

"Can you keep a secret?"

"You must go to your grave with this."

"If you need to lie under oath, do it."

"You're special."

"I noticed you."

"You're different."

Like a magnet, these statements pull you in, wrapping you up in a disguise of acceptance. My abuser was setting the stage of my cage. We need acceptance to be included and chosen. Mine was extreme control: clothing, friendships, activities, having to keep so many secrets.

This playlist of untruths stopped the day I found my voice and spoke the truth.

If you're in church leadership, report to the proper authorities. Help the victim feel included in your circle of protection, not excluded and shamed. Immoral leadership may use brainwashing, fear, rules that propel their agenda, the misused authority of scripture, unholy hierarchy, spy tactics, and—most of all—take advantage of the natural needs and weaknesses of its members to create an environment that serves the leadership's needs at the expense of everyone else.

What you can do now: identify one "untruth" you've believed about yourself because of your experience. Write it down now, then write a biblical truth that counters it.

Finding True Belonging and Healing

Do you have a place in your heart that longs to be filled?

Perhaps you've reached and searched for belonging, to be valued. We were created to belong and to be accepted. You may have searched at school, at home, at work and—yes— even at church. To be loved is to belong. It's natural to get lost and found in a relationship. The difficulties are all part of the journey.

However, if you aren't safe, this isn't love. This makes you feel all alone. Your heart deserves to be cherished and valued.

My expedition of discovery to belong took me twenty-nine years. I found my husband, and ten years later, I discovered my inner emptiness when I told him my whole story. My husband finally heard and understood me. Forty years later, I found my voice as my Savior lovingly destroyed the locks on my cage, one by one.

Has false and abusive love wounded you? Wounds of love, whether pure or tainted, run deep. Many haven't recovered from these wounds. I felt wounded, with a deep sense of loss and no will to live, but Jesus rescued me. There's hope!

People poked my scars in disbelief, asking, "Are you 'sure' it was rape?" I'm not hiding them anymore. My scars are now a sign of healing from trauma.

I want to guide you toward the right treatment for your wounds. It may sting, but the medicine cleans and helps to heal. You may have to take a moment and catch your breath because the pain is unbearable. Let the medicine do its work. I'll walk with you.

What you can do now: Find one small daily practice that makes you feel safe and connected (prayer, journaling, calling a trusted friend). Commit to this practice for one week.

Reclaiming Your Life

Has the abuse caused you to react destructively?

Punishing yourself, blaming yourself, or hurting yourself by escaping from those who want to rescue you is harmful to you and your mental health. Maybe you haven't considered that this could be a reaction on your part to surviving.

Those who've been abused take on this noble effort: "I mustn't tell: I must protect those around me." It's a lie to think that you carry an insurmountable burden. That's what I did. I carried it for decades.

Let me gently remind you again; it's not your fault.

My husband and my boys told me I needed help. My first step was shaky, but I did it. I sought professional help. A mental breakdown was imminent after confiding to my husband and sons. I couldn't carry this anymore.

Someone unlocked Pandora's box, releasing all the secrets I'd padlocked behind a heavy door. Triggers left and right, from smells to movies. Uncontrollable episodes of crying, haunting dreams in which I'd wake up screaming—my tucked away memories were unfettering themselves. Weight loss, and heaviness of heart—these were all destructive to my physical and mental health.

Like relentless weeds popping up in a vibrant and colorful flower garden, my "perfect" flower garden needed a deep root evacuation.

It was time to deal with my trauma.

I wasn't alone in my recovery. My husband, boys, and dearest friends have been cheering me on. I still lament my wasted years, but my Jesus has put people in my life to pray with me and for me, to assist me, to walk with me, cry with me and laugh. Genuine family and friends will choose to love you. In their eyes, you'll never need to merit their affection and trust. Surround yourself with these precious humans.

My poem on the next page reflects my families rescue of me. When I was in my darkest place, they reached out to me and helped pull me out.

Light in the Darkness (From Victim to Victors)

My Jesus set me free
He gave me a place for sheltered rest, next to Him.
I *have* traded my secrets for His secret place.
My *heart is* brimming with His love.
I pray this transforming love fills your heart.
It can happen!
I am a witness.
Jesus is the Great Light.
He came to my dark cave, found me caged, locked
with deceitful lies.
He revealed this perverted and warped love.
He showed me nothing corrupts His love, His truth.
I could trust that *it is* pure and spotless.
Truth found me, and that was Jesus.
I have the key to your locked cage.
Love
Yes, genuine love
This overwhelming love of God chased me down.
Rescued me.
I was lost in the shadows of deceit and disillusion.
Hid, in the darkness of my cave, my Savior came.
He can uncover your locked cage.
Removing the cloak of shame, fear and filth.
May His light penetrate your vast darkness.
My glimmer of hope bounced off the key to redemption.
Jesus held this key in His nail-scarred hand.
It read, LOVE.
Can you hear the clicks of the locks being opened?
He dresses our wounds and scars with His oil of joy.
This oil of joy is immeasurable and never ending.
We are wrapped in His garment of praise, I can see
the Light, can you?
Let's walk together, as Jesus leads the way.
May we never forget, Jesus is our truth, and HE sets us free.

— Bridget Goodwin, 2025

Our faith is increased and healed when we reflect on the words that Jesus spoke and John captured these illuminating words: *"And you shall know the truth, and the truth will set you free."* (John 8:32, ESV).

What you can do now: Consider what healthy spirituality might look like for you now. What aspects of faith bring comfort rather than fear? Make note of these as anchors for your journey. Also, identify one safe person who might walk with you on this healing journey. Consider reaching out to them or preparing what you might say when you're ready. Join our community, we provide guided support for having these important conversations safely.

My Song of Freedom to Guide You towards Your Voice

Because of this rescue, I found my voice. I'm going to guide you through the same proven process that helped survivors reclaim their voices. I want to sing my song with you. Let this poem be our battle cry, let's sing together, "I have a voice!"

I Have a Voice

You thought you could silence me forever, but I *have*
found my voice.
Just like a bird, I *have* found my song.
I will sing this song; *I will* let the melodious strain be
heard near and far.
This song will be sad and joyful, each note adding to
the story, the story of my healing, my redemption,
and deliverance.
This *healing is* hope for all who listen.
It is a message of safety for women, daughters and sons.
We can arise from the heap of heartaches, abuse, and
terror.
Each stone laid on top of our lives, removed one by one.
Deliverance from the chains that hold us captive to
our past.
The Cross, the redemptive flow of Christ's crimson
blood, has been shed for my story to be redeemed
and my life restored, and forgiveness for my assailant.
I sing my song, the song of redeeming grace, my
chains are gone, I've been set free from my captive,
my cage has been opened.
I have my voice. I shall fly!

— Bridget Goodwin, 2021

It's never too late for you! I've seen young and old find their
voice. I've listened to men and women share their stories and
start their healing journey. Age isn't a barrier!

Your quest has started, and I'll give you guidance if you
allow me. As we unfurl the map to the road of recovery, we'll
track down your voice.

Why I'm Sharing This with You Now

Simply put, I want to see you set free, and transformed.

I want healing.

I want redemption.

For whom?

For those who've lost their voice, me included. If I can keep my story from being repeated, I've succeeded. Everyone locked in a cage can be free with the key of LOVE.

My voice is one of restoration and redemption. I want you to be heard and understood, too.

If you're a victim, there's hope. May you be wholly blessed and loved for who you truly are, without pretense or precondition. I know this is going to be arduous, but I'm on this expedition with you.

You may have suffered sexual abuse from your mother, father, sister, brother, uncle, aunt, grandma, grandpa, colleague, stranger, pastor, or clergy member. This is grim indeed. Molestation is the unhealthiest kind of touching there is. It's about taking and not giving. It's about putting on shackles: not a thriving atmosphere for giving assurance to live and be free.

Since my release, I've hoped to keep the "one" (those who may find themselves in a precarious situation or an alert system to be set in place in your life of awareness of the danger) free from this happening to them. Innocence forever preserved, life untouched or harmed. My words are for you, as well, the "one" that I pray will grow into many. I hope to deliver you or keep you from repeating my story of abuse— then my story will be worth it.

This is also for those who have a friend, family member, or a loved one who's a victim of sexual trauma who's been silenced. My desire is to give you an insight into exiting the labyrinth of abuse. You'll know how to support and understand.

I've changed the names and places of abuse. When I use initials or pseudo names, they don't represent actual names. My abusers are dead. I've no desire to defame their families nor those who were enablers, knowingly or unknowingly. God will judge as He sees fit. My name is real. It's my voice and I'm not hiding anymore.

Let me share how a vibrant, innocent girl lost her voice and found it again. The years of abuse changed my voice. It became distorted, silenced. From the lovely strains of a bird, free to fly, to a dull, trapped parakeet repeating commands. But I transformed into a dove, free to fly high in the sky. Why? Because I found my voice, so listen to me sing.

This is for you. You may see yourself as the victim, but I'm going to help you become a victor.

What you can do now: Consider your own healing journey. What would one small step forward look like for you? Perhaps it's reading the next chapter, reaching out to a friend, or simply acknowledging your pain. Whatever it is, know that you don't walk alone.

From California to Iowa, I'll take you back to where my story began—the church community that should've protected me but didn't. You'll learn how to recognize the warning signs I missed and understand the systematic manipulation tactics used by predators in religious settings. More importantly, you'll begin to see how these same patterns may have appeared in your own experience.

The journey ahead won't be easy. There may be moments when you'll need to set this book aside and breathe. That's okay—healing isn't linear.

But I promise you this: if you stay with me, page by page, you'll discover that your voice—though perhaps just a whisper now—will grow stronger. By the end of this book, you'll have the same proven five-step framework that can transform your life as it has for others.

Turn the page when you're ready. I'll be waiting for you on the other side.

CHAPTER 2
California to Iowa

Give me the sun, sand and the sea, let me fly and soak in the rays of the warm sun, to the serenade of the waves, beckoning me to stay." – Bridget

✝

I remember days in the sun—Mom and Dad packing up the car, heading to the beach for the weekend on Dad's day off. We'd stop at the corner store on the way, where he'd buy a bag of Cheetos and punch with little foil caps for me and my little brother. Mom would wash me in the kitchen sink when we returned home to rinse all the sand off me. Days of fun and freedom—that's how I recall California.

Christmas was always full of wonder. Big glowing Christmas lights of blue, red, yellow and orange with twinkling tinsel thrown on the boughs of the fragrant fir tree. A plastic Santa and Frosty the Snowman lit up the living room, nestled on top of the TV cabinet. Shining ornaments that magnified your face when you peered into them, and TV shows of "Rudolph the Red-Nosed Reindeer" with Burl Ives' lovely, rich voice narrating—two little kids waiting for the big day. Palm trees, sunshine and warmth—these were my Christmases.

Birthdays brought go-go shorts, Snow White and the Seven Dwarfs birthday cake, a Malibu Barbie doll, blowing out the candles and celebrating with my grandma, Mom, and my little brother. These were the delightful days of my formative years.

Kindergarten meant walking to school with Mom and my brother—a journey that seemed endless, crossing the water levies, passing the Thrifty store. All sweet memories. Painting with colors on black construction paper, big chunky crayons, gluing beads and macaroni on paper—the smells of paint, crayons and glue all create splendid memories.

I dressed up for Halloween as a gypsy with a big colorful scarf wrapped around my little five-year-old body, wearing big costume rings on my tiny fingers. I sang Christmas carols and memorized my one line—" while sugarplums danced in their heads"—from the school production of "The Night Before Christmas."

Going to church with my Mormon Grandma B. meant playing in the nursery, drinking from the little paper cup for communion and eating the little morsel of white bread. I'd stay up late with Grandma B., falling asleep watching "Hollywood Squares." Riding in my Grandpa B.'s car, I listened to Dean Martin's crooning, velvety voice on his 8-track tape. These are all part of the wonderful memories of childhood.

My Mom would sew cotton dresses for me. I remember sinking my nose into the fabric, smelling the crisp, rich cotton. Vibrant prints of Holly Hobbie and, later, one flowing double-knit dress I loved to twirl around in.

Why Do the Good Memories Matter?

For me, the nostalgia of my childhood is endearing, sweet, and delightful. You could stop here and reminisce, perhaps longing to stay in these moments. Yet life happens—the good, the bad, the ugly and the beautiful. As a grown-up, you learn to hold on to the treasures and let go of the counterfeit items that try to appear as truth. You discover that these are only illusions.

These special moments of my early days are like love letters, tucked away in my memory bank.

As I continue my story, the interweaving of the good and the bad will become very apparent. Just like a tapestry, each thread is important to the overall texture of beauty and color in the final image. The view from the backside is ugly— muddled, confusing, disorganized, and chaotic.

My value and treasured love becomes twisted, perverted, and malformed. I will flip the art piece around and show you the image coming to life: my rescue, my redemption, my quest for genuine love, and how I discovered this love.

What I understand now, is that these precious memories aren't just nostalgia—they're proof of your authentic self. When trauma tries to convince you that darkness is all there is, these moments become anchors to who you really are. They remind you that joy, safety, and love are your birthright, not the abuse you endured.

Years later, I wrote these words trying to reach back to that girl—the one who rode her bike into the California sunset, the one who still lives inside me today.

California Girl

I listened to these sweet lyrics today, my heart
saddened at this innocent girl that was once me.
Loving life in the warm rays of the southwest, riding
my bike into the dusk, reflectors glowing in the lights
of the early evenings.
Escaping to the corner at the end of our street, with
my brother on our bikes, buying candy at the Elks
Club, chewing it and spitting it out before we arrived
back home, a bit giddy, thinking Mom never knew.
Oh, these sweet innocent days of wonder and
discovery, California days.
The sun, sand and sea, happy memories for me.
My Mom, sewing my clothes with her own hands, the
crisp cotton that I loved to sink my nose in, colorful
patterns. I wore these threads with pride.
My Dad, working hard, shifts back-to-back, me and
my brother, stealing a sip from his iced cold Pepsi that
was sitting on the table, dinner before that afternoon shift.
Warm days outside, playing in the mud, making mud
pies with little discarded tiles, chasing each other,
playing hide and seek at night with friends, the night
fragrant with night blooming jasmine,
This was my California, my years of innocence.
I'm reminded, this little girl, hair pulled back, face
glowing, kissed by the sun, sitting on her royal blue
Schwinn bike, is still inside me today.
I just need to find her....
God sees me as this adventurous little girl, and it's
time for Him to "restore all that I thought was lost".
I will get back on that bike, I will pedal into the sunset,
wind blowing my grey streaked hair, my face now
creased with age, but I will glow, yes, I have scars, but
I will always be that California girl, a child, His daughter.

—Bridget Goodwin, 2021

The Choice That Saved Me Before I Was Born

I was born in the late '60s in sunny California. I'm still astounded—as others may think likewise—that my parents' teenage love would have lasted over fifty-eight years! This puppy love turned into me, a love child. Free love has its choices and consequences.

My young, unmarried father had to make a choice. They encouraged adoption. This was an option, but it would mean rejection for me. Maybe this would have been the best for two struggling teenagers trying to survive in this thing called "the real world"?

How do you deal with an unplanned birth?

Would they abandon me before I could be in my biological mother's arms?

Could my father turn his back on me and put me up for adoption?

Adoption is the answer for some cases—a rescue for some that's beneficial for the welfare of the child, or young adult. I'm sure my father contemplated all the consequences. Maybe the family wanted to be rid of this dilemma, which was me.

My parents wanted me, so they got married. However, there was a problem—they were underage. My Grandpa comes to the rescue and gives his permission for his sixteen-year-old daughter to marry her seventeen-year-old boyfriend. I attended my parents' wedding as a baby bump under the lovely flowing white dress of my very young and gorgeous Mom. I was born four months later.

However, tragedy struck—I was born with a hole in my heart. The diagnosis from the doctor was grim. My father drowned out the future predicted by the medical statistics with prayer. The strong faith of his mother shaped his prayers that day. "If you would heal my daughter, I will give her to you." Little did I know that this prayer had a trajectory like an arrow shooting toward my destiny. At my follow-up, doctors found my heart healed.

> **What you can do now:** Consider what aspects of your younger self you might need to reclaim. What qualities or joys did you once possess that deserve to be restored? Write these down to remind yourself that healing often involves recovering what was lost.

When Love Wasn't Enough

My father was not a saved man. Even though my physical heart healed, I developed an emotional hole in my deepest self. My parents fought, argued, and yelled. They struggled like every newlywed with a little one. The noise of their arguments scared me, so I would hide behind the chair. Nothing could drown out the disturbance and the turmoil I felt. My gaping hole in my soul thrived in this environment. My father worked long hours to cover the deficit in our household. He carried this weight without faltering, providing for his family. My parents nurtured me as much as they could.

But where was the love for my growing hole in my heart?

Could I survive with my dad never being home?

Could these two teenagers survive the transition from puppy love to real love that drives you to make family relationships work?

I think this is why I hold the memories of the weekend beach trips with so much fondness. These trips were like a salve for my heart. Time with my dad and mom, the surf lapping at my little chubby feet, and the sun driving away the dark clouds in my little heart. Family togetherness, laughing and enjoying a surf-side charcoal-fired hamburger—priceless.

Our family of three grew to four when my brother was born. I was annoyed by this little bundle called my brother. Saturated with meanness, I took it out on him. I pulled out his umbilical cord. I pushed him down the cement stairs in his baby carrier. This hole in my heart made me lack love and care. Was it my environment and the turmoil in my life?

Things were deteriorating. Mom had already separated from my dad when my brother was born. The duties of a young mother took a toll on her young marriage. Her voice longed to be heard. Yet I never remember my dad not being part of our lives. One night he came home, and something happened that changed our lives forever.

This emotional emptiness, this desperate need for love and attention, is what made me vulnerable to what was coming. I now understand that predators have a radar for this kind of need. They can sense when someone is hungry for love, attention, or belonging—and they use it against them. Understanding this pattern isn't about blame; it's about recognizing how trauma makes us susceptible to further manipulation.

The Night Everything Changed

One of my dad's co-workers had shared—just through his lifestyle—that he had found Jesus, and my dad could see that this had turned this young man's life around. This moved my dad so much that he wanted this Jesus too. I'm sure my Pentecostal Grandma E. had prayed many prayers over my father. My father grew up in a split home. He learned to survive with just him and his older brother. This created a very strong-willed and hardworking young man. Nothing could pierce this hardened heart but the love of Jesus.

Dad's co-workers invited my dad to their church. At the altar call, he hesitated, knowing that not going forward meant the end. He needed this love. He needed redemption for his detrimental ways. His marriage was falling apart. These thoughts whirled in his mind. Church was over, and he steps forward, grabs my mom, and gives his life to Jesus at the altar. Salvation's glorious light transformed his face. He tells Mom she needs this in her life. She follows Jesus too.

Little did I know that as my brother and I ran between the aisles of the pews at that little white church in Anaheim, my world was getting ready to change for the better. Mom was getting ready to leave Dad. She'd had enough. But that night in December, a few days before Christmas, my dad and mom were born again—and that redeemed them and their marriage.

So much sentiment surrounds Christmas. Perhaps it's because this marked the time that my home life changed, and I at last felt safe in my family of four. When I was five years old, I remember my father's glorious transformation.

His outward appearance reflected his conversion. He sang, he prayed, he was happy! He stopped the habits that were deteriorating his life and marriage. My little eyes could see and my ears could hear that my dad was different. The fighting stopped. We had peace in the home. This exchange of turmoil to peace tugged at my heart. I wanted what my father had. My dad became a missionary in his own home. I wanted to change; I wanted his Jesus.

My heart broke for my mean ways. I was so convicted for months. At six years old, I was born again—this made me so happy. The "hole" in my heart healed. I found Jesus and His love, which my gaping "hole" yearned for. When you really experience Jesus, you will never be the same.

My mom told me I had changed. I wanted to be nice to my little brother. I wanted to be like my dad. The promissory note of prayer from my father when I was born came true. Dad gave me to Jesus, but actually Jesus came for me. This intimate relationship with my Savior would carry me through many dark and dangerous valleys in the years ahead.

My California Church Home: Finding Community

My dad was so very protective of me. Public schools in the '70s were becoming unsafe and increasingly frightening for me. Bullies targeted me for wearing dresses, and girls from gangs harassed me. I so wanted to have friends and to be engaged with after-school activities. I loved art and music, but my father limited my after-school functions. This created a loneliness for a child of my age. My best friend outside of school was my little brother.

Young families filled the sweet little church we attended, and I loved being with them. Of course, they were mostly older, and I'm sure I was more of an annoyance than a joy! But it's so very special that they would include me.

I adored our little church, and they quickly became my family. My family gave all their free time to help build the new church and make it thrive. My dad cared for the property as we lived on the premises. Mom learned how to sew.

My best memories of church are here, in California. Hide and seek at night on the church property with the fragrance of night-blooming jasmine filling my nostrils as I sought for a place to hide. My shimmering blue Schwinn bike was my companion day in and day out. Fun days and nights in the warm, balmy air of California. Learning how to play the cornet was so enjoyable for me. I was finding my voice, and music became a refuge of healing and nurturing that I escaped to in later, sadder days.

They founded the little church school after finishing the new building, and I attended sixth and seventh grade there. No more gangs. I thrived in this environment. I may not have had friends my age, but I was part of the people who loved my mom and dad at the beginning of their walk with the Lord. No church is perfect, but the early days here were blissful.

What you can do now: Create a brief list of places where you've felt safe and truly accepted. Consider how you might incorporate elements of these safe spaces into your current healing journey.

The Charismatic Visitor: The First Warning Signs

But then, things changed. A respected teacher over a group of churches from the Midwest visited our little congregation. My father was already aware of this dynamic preacher because he'd read some of his teachings that were formatted into books. Our pastor invited him to our church dedication over Thanksgiving. My father was smitten by this powerful leader and his charismatic ways.

How quickly this new father figure invaded the privacy of his current pastor—the one who took my father in and gave him love, value and fatherly attention. My dad instantly responds with regard and respect to this man, placing him on a pedestal. Already, this man that I will call "Perseus" lures him away from the loyalty of his father in the Lord. This man's toxic attention gives my dad a false sense of specialness.

I enter the scene, just a child of eight or nine. He singles me out immediately. "Oh, you are Brother Greg's daughter." I can still remember this attention. He even tells my mom in the dining room that he wants to take me home with him! My mom quickly told him that my brother and I were bookends—he would have to take both of us.

This man disrupted our lives and my little "home" church. He even wanted to take a picture of me with him. Even at this very young age, I remember how his wife disliked me and this picture being taken.

Perseus wanted to visit our home, but our pastor heard about it, and it troubled him. My father listened to his pastor, but this does not stop Perseus. He pulled on my father through phone calls and printed materials.

The rift began.

This relentless man pulled my father's heart. I will call our pastor "Pastor Parson." Pastor Parson showed unmeasured love and compassion to my mom and dad. Pastor Parson and his wife graciously and mercifully met the needs of all new believers in Jesus, including their need for the importance of mentoring and nurturing in lifestyle changes. They saw what was happening with Perseus and heeded the warning signs.

Looking back now, Perseus displayed every classic sign of a predatory leader. We must learn to recognize these manipulation tactics because they're so common in religious settings. The way he immediately singled me out, expressed inappropriate interest in taking me away from my parents, and systematically drove a wedge between my father and his trusted pastor—these aren't coincidences. They're calculated moves in a predator's playbook.

What you can do now: Trust your instincts. Reflect on a time when you felt uncomfortable around someone but dismissed your feelings. How might honoring these intuitive responses help protect you in the future?

Leaving California—And Losing Myself

Despite Pastor Parson's concerns, Perseus succeeds. My family is now taking a trip to the Midwest to visit the grand opening of his new church and big congregation. My first plane ride, my first time out of state, our first family vacation for more than a few days.

I'm now thirteen years old. These meetings were paramount to the "special" Christians, the so-called "elite," a "selection from the selection." It was exhilarating for me—so many new things to discover in this flat land of the Midwest.

I played my cornet in this forty-piece band, a musical haven for me. I made a friend right away. We roamed the enormous halls that still smelled of new carpet after dinner time, waiting for the evening service.

The sanctuary was vast—dark blue carpet on the floor, shiny polished walnut paneling that lined the walls, white stuccoed walls with curved lines reaching up to the light wood squares of the ceilings held by big walnut beams that looked like arches. The soft light blue upholstered pews with walnut trim—the place of worship just swallowed me up. It was inviting and intoxicating at the same time.

Back in California, things speed up toward this upheaval of change. Pastor Parson was not a fan of Perseus and his teachings. Perseus was actually working toward taking my family away from our first love, our first home church. In desperation, Pastor Parson made an ultimatum in church, and my family, along with several other families, walked out the opened doors. My dad made a choice, and we followed. As soon as we arrived home, I remember my dad grabbing the phone and its long cord and taking it to a private room. He was calling Perseus.

The next couple of days were a whirlwind of events. My mother, myself, and my little brother board an airplane for the Midwest with only our suitcases. We were leaving my beloved California. A bold step for my family. My father thought moving us would solve several things. If we stayed in California, I might have to go back to public school. I'd suffered violence in this environment—a broken eardrum from a student hitting me in class and bullying. The progressive ways were already bleeding into the school system. New school, new church, new friends and new state— it seemed time to start over.

My father had already established his own business, so he had to stay behind and sell the business that he'd built up from scratch. Maybe he felt that sending us ahead secured the spot for him to make this transition to be in the "special group." It was so urgent for us to move. One month later, Dad packs up with only a trailer to give us a better life elsewhere. He left behind so many things.

I left my freedom behind the day I boarded the plane. Leaving my sky-blue Schwinn bike should have been a red flag. They did not allow bikes in this new church. No more wind blowing in my face as I pedaled into the sunset of California. The days of my sweet innocence were forever gone.

What you can do now: Consider times when someone else quickly influenced you to make major life decisions. What questions might have been helpful to ask during these transitions? How can you ensure your future decisions are made carefully?

If you're reading this and recognizing similar patterns in your own life—someone pushing you to make major changes quickly, isolating you from support systems, or making you feel special while undermining your other relationships— please know that help is available. Let me provide a safe space for you to explore these concerns without judgment.

The End of Innocence

That blue Schwinn bike represented more than transportation—it represented choice, freedom, and the right to go where I wanted. In the controlling world I was about to enter, such choices would be systematically stripped away. But here's what I know now that I didn't know then: even when our freedom is taken, the desire for it never truly dies. It waits, sometimes for decades, for the moment when we can claim it again.

I had no idea that this move to Iowa would change everything, I thought California sunshine would last forever. I had no idea the Midwest would become my cage.

I'll take you into the controlling world I entered when we moved to the Midwest. You'll learn how gradually, seemingly small restrictions became a cage that trapped not just me, but our entire family. The contrast between my free California days and what was to come is stark—and understanding this progression is crucial for recognizing similar patterns in religious settings today.

The California girl inside me never completely disappeared, even in the darkest times ahead. She waited, sometimes silently, for the day when she could ride free again. And if you're reading this, that girl inside you is waiting too.

Red Flags: Spot Spiritual Manipulation

These patterns of manipulation appeared early in my story and often exist in religious environments where abuse occurs:

1. Charismatic authority figures:
- Commanding unusual levels of respect/admiration
- Generating intense emotional responses
- People placed on a pedestal

2. Inappropriate attention toward children:
- Singling out specific children for special attention
- Expressing unusual interest in taking a child away from parents
- Requesting photos or mementos of specific children

3. Boundary violations:
- Attempting to visit family's home despite objections
- Persistent contact through calls after initial advances are rebuffed
- Undermining existing relationships (like Perseus did with Pastor Parson)

4. Division and isolation:
- Creating divisions within communities
- Forcing people to choose sides
- Separating families from supportive communities

5. Urgency and pressure:
- Rapid, pressured decision-making about major life changes; sudden relocations
- Leaving possessions behind
- Feeling compelled to decide quickly to please an authority figure

CHAPTER 3
The "Group"

"Like a flame mesmerized a moth, I flew right into my cage, unaware that I would burn." – Bridget

†

Through my healing and working with survivors, I've learned that religious predators follow a predictable playbook. They understand our deepest human needs—for belonging, purpose, and spiritual connection—and they weaponize these needs to create dependency. What I'm about to share isn't just my story; it's a case study in how spiritual manipulation unfolds.

At thirteen, I didn't realize I was being lured into a trap. The massive sanctuary with its dim lights and riveting music wasn't just impressive—it seemed to be designed to overwhelm and attract. What I experienced as community was actually the beginning of systematic control.

It is my mission to help survivors find these patterns of manipulation early on. Early recognition is key to protection.

Let me show you how it worked, so you can recognize these patterns before they ensnare you or someone you love.

The Seduction: Creating Irresistible Attraction

Predators know effective manipulation starts with genuine charm. They create an environment that meets real needs while establishing the foundation for future control.

It was so easy to get lost in the massive church sanctuary. The dim lights that glowed before the weekly church service beckoned you to find a seat in one of the many pews that lined the church building from front to back. However, the leaders encouraged you to sit up front, where the action took place, giving you a clear view of the pulpit where the 'man of God' delivered his sermon.

The music was big and riveting, from the sonorous sound of the brass to the soft harmonies of the woodwinds. A heavy bass rhythm held all the voices in balance. The direction came from the pianist with the organ following right along. This harmonious sound pulled and allured me. It comforted me as I tried to belong.

I have learned that this systematic sensory overload can overwhelm you, designed to create emotional vulnerability. When people feel moved by music and atmosphere, they're more likely to accept what follows without critical thinking. It is so important to define the difference between God's presence and hyped emotionalism.

I have felt the deep moves of God in the very quiet moments of worship and in the joyous shouts of praise through voice and song. God's Spirit nurtures us, inspires us to walk closer to Him, changes us for the better—for transformation. Worship nurtures this relationship with Jesus and our Heavenly Father.

We were created with emotions, and we can get caught away in the moment, but what happens after determines if it was God or the unity of sound in the moment. Just like a sports event—moving, almost spine tingling, everyone chanting for their team.

Only the Holy Spirit can witness to you what is not counterfeit, but real.

Membership in the 'mother' church held a special and distinguished status. They used the term 'bride member' for this special group. 144,000 was His beloved, His bride, that leaned on His bosom.

"A selection from a selection."

"The 99, not the one."

"Cream of the crop."

"100 fold, not the 30."

I see this exclusionary language in every controlling religious system I've studied. It's a classic manipulation tactic that creates artificial scarcity and competition for belonging.

This was the benchmark of our standing with the 'elite.' Reservations were required, and the ministry held your RSVP, not you. You must deserve this place through your outward works and allegiance to the 'ministry.' No questions asked. They considered submission to mean you had what they considered to be 'the right spirit.' This celebration of your bridal party would be on the other side—in your eternal life.

What a difference for me to find a place to grow outside of my little 'homegrown' church of California. So many more members, no distinction of social statuses, all dressing well. These people acted 'special.' The leader monopolized the pulpit. It was normal for there to be hours upon hours of teaching. Three times a week, we listened to this animated and powerful man. What I now recognize as indoctrination through repetition—a technique designed to overwhelm critical thinking through constant exposure to one voice, one perspective.

The widow that we would end up staying with was part of this promotion of endless hours of teaching. She had 'special tapes'—ones that were not edited from every service where Perseus preached to his congregation. She kept these special tapes, recorded on her own tape recorder, in her possession; the recorder sat beside her in the pew. No one else could record the church services.

Names were called out for lessons of how not to be. These were individuals who were not complying with the rules set by Perseus. These were the rebels. The 'bride' knew better. All of us learned how to judge these rebels from the berating words that came from the pulpit. Why this widow had her own recordings and could distribute these in secret was a mystery.

In the PA booth, the services were recorded—but the tapes were edited to remove the denunciations. The library offered these tapes for checkout and home use, as if we hadn't already had enough at church. Only the church library provided edited tapes. The church encouraged every home to listen to the tapes. Only those who attended church heard the names being called. Love is to honor and uplift. Name calling is intimidating, threatening and humiliating. I shudder to think of the brainwashing that filled our homes as the tapes played over and over.

I learned to walk in step with everyone, trying to be part of this 'group.'

Through my own healing, I've realized that churches shouldn't use control, surveillance, or threats. We must learn how to see these toxic behaviors of an individual, a group or even a cultish church. We must see how this desperate need to belong makes us vulnerable to accepting treatment we would normally reject.

What you can do now: Reflect on communities where you've felt a strong desire to belong. What healthy aspects of belonging felt nurturing? What unhealthy aspects might have created pressure to conform? Write three qualities of the genuine community you want in your life.

Financial Control: Testing Compliance Through Sacrifice

Financial control is often the first major test of compliance. Predators know that if they can get you to sacrifice basic needs for the organization, they can control everything else.

My mother was a pioneer. She left everything—her possessions, her family, and life in California to pave the way for my dad to arrive. We stayed with a widowed woman. It wasn't easy for us. Mom had to give the funds Dad provided for us to this widow. The widow instructed her to tithe the first portion of the funds to the church.

The widow rationed the food, and even the bathwater had to be shared. This systematic deprivation while maintaining financial obligations to the church is designed to create total dependency. The control was starting. Everything was being reported to the ministry. I did not know how much my mom suffered. All I remember is how she had to discipline us: the food ration, the shared bath water, and what we had to pack for lunch. I was so embarrassed by the lack evidenced in our lunches.

In my healing work, I've seen this same pattern of financial control used to trap dozens of families. The formula is always the same: create artificial scarcity while demanding continued financial commitment to the organization.

However, even in this controlled environment I was happy. I was starting to have friends within the church, and that seemed to balance the odd way of life for me and my brother.

Another change: my mom needed to work, a bold step. She had always been at home for me and my brother. The only work that would fit her skill set was at the men's department, altering clothing. The church enforced instructions about tithing, giving until it hurts. This came before the needs of lodging, food and clothing. Mom had to do her part—tithes and school tuition.

Almost a month passed, and my dad arrived after his long drive from California. The leaves had changed in the Midwest and the sight was one of the most glorious things I had ever seen. The leaves were beckoning to me that life was changing. Brilliant colors begged to be admired. I pointed out this spectacular show with gasps of wonder. I had never experienced such an array of colors. I had lived in an arid, palm tree environment. Another life change unfolded before me. I didn't realize that it wasn't all beautiful and brilliant.

The problem was that, having arrived at last, Dad couldn't find a job. The church came first. He must pay tithes and school tuition. I experienced poverty in our family for the first time. My father had left his thriving business to make this move. The 'group' offered no help and nurturing. This 'giving until it hurts' was the payment of our love, money and submission. Mom was now the sole provider.

What healthy spiritual communities understand is that love resembles giving—from the community to those in need, not extracting resources from struggling families.

What you can do now: Consider how people can use financial pressure as a control mechanism. If you've experienced financial manipulation in a church setting, identify one boundary you can establish to protect yourself financially in the future.

Voice Suppression and Rule Enforcement

I teach that authentic expression is a target of control systems. They understand that once they can control your voice, they can control your identity.

During this tumultuous time of fitting in, Dad found employment. It was not his vocation from California. He had to start all over and go back to school. We adjusted, and it seemed that I thrived in the school. My voice was heard in the chapel services on Wednesday morning. I sang, worshipped and testified.

The hole in my heart was being filled with God's presence that I was encountering. I was zealous. I wanted to share His goodness. What I now recognize is that they noted this authentic spiritual expression and immediately moved to control it. A school monitor pulled me aside into the cloakroom to advise me to restrain my eagerness. This was so strange. I had to be controlled. My voice learned that it had to have permission.

The systematic stifling of genuine expression is present in every case of spiritual abuse I've seen. When genuine spiritual gifts threaten their control, they reframe it as a problem that needs correction.

Others gave me clothing. Shoes and dresses, but you would never find trousers in these brown bags. They didn't let women and girls wear trousers. I was getting ready to experience the snow for the first time, but in a skirt! Frigid temperatures with only a coat and boots to combat these subzero wind chills. Sledding never happened for me in the Midwest. They didn't allow me to do that. That's okay because I treasure the memories of sledding at Big Bear Lake Snow Resort in the San Bernardino Mountains in California with my first church family.

For as long as I could remember, my mom made most of my clothes. We chose patterns and fabric together. How freeing it was to have these moments with my mother deciding which pattern, what fabric, which buttons and ribbon we would choose for my new outfit.

I came to the Midwest with these handmade threads. But my flowing homemade dresses also came under scrutiny. I was not to wear unbelted dresses; those were only for pregnant women.

What was I to do? My parents could not afford a new wardrobe for me. The clothes given to me weren't sufficient, nor did they suit me. I found some twine and made a belt. So, another chain was added to my bondage. This time it was clothing. Looking back, I can see that this was not an attempt to impose modesty but rather to accentuate my developing body. Charm classes at school reiterated the restrictive dress code. Girdle for girls, long sleeves, hose—even if you wore tennis shoes for PE—hair not cut, checked regularly by staff, skirts below the knee. Absolutely no make-up and simple hairstyles only.

Controlling systems understand that when they can dictate personal choices like clothing, they're establishing dominance over identity itself.

Love is rich... and it's free. This price of being included required us to meet the cost. Genuine spiritual community celebrates authentic expression rather than requiring conformity.

What you can do now: Consider how unhealthy environments use genuine talent or spiritual gifts as both reward and control. Reflect on how a controlling setting misused your genuine gifts, and how you might reclaim them healthily.

The Trap Closes: Rewards and Entrapment

What I've learned through my work with survivors is that the final stage of entrapment involves giving just enough rewards to make victims feel special while closing off all escape routes.

After several months, I must have been pleasing the pastor with my submission and devotion. I was finally allowed to join the church band with my trumpet. I had been asking since I moved. For a 13-year-old, this was a top honor. I was being watched. I passed the test.

Trinkets—including the honor of serving—dazzled me, although I failed to notice the chains of ensnarement enveloping me. What I now understand is that these rewards were calculated to increase my investment in the system. I believed they selected, included, and honored me, but I had been blinded. I did not know this, but I was being singled out—noticed, watched, and contemplated. My once-open cage was being decorated with chains that locked me in. Bar by bar, they—he—added to my cage, my prison. Each one representing the price being paid for the perks of being part of the 'group.'

My compliance with their rules and my elevation was necessary for my survival. I wanted to be united with this 'group' because, after all, the role of the 'bride' was reserved only for the special ones. The brainwashing—the dizzying back-and-forth of duties, corrections and honors—became a way of life for me and consumed me.

The price was that I was being taught how to comply and, through this education, I became lost. My attendance at church four times a week, all in my spare time, my submission to all their rules. The replacement of my parents' authority with the pastor, and even the control over what clothes I wore, were all sacrificed on the altar of commitment. This systematic compliance training was a form of psychological conditioning designed to eliminate critical thinking.

Incendiary condemnations of those who dared to flaunt even the smallest rules saturated sermons and fireside chats. From the pulpit, we were constantly told that 'sheep are dumb.' And, like sheep, we were told to follow the middle— the golden center—veering neither to one side nor the other.

Predators understand that impossible standards create perpetual insecurity. We were told that the 'man of God' was pulling and pushing a pendulum, expecting we would find this middle. But how could we? The middle only existed in his mind, and whatever we decided was the middle never quite matched his definition of it. Week in and week out, he sacrificed us like lambs before the altar, furiously criticizing us in front of our friends and family for failing to find this mysterious middle. No one was exempt, except maybe himself, from these bruising and blistering messages, which he had supposedly found in God's loving Word.

The middle was nowhere to be found. No one was worthy of defying this middle. The rules themselves remained a mystery.

These unanswerable questions are designed to create dependency. When you can never be sure you're doing it right, you become completely dependent on the leader's approval. The church as a congregation thought the answer was to note whom not to follow, and draw yourself away from them. If they went to the altar to repent and return, then it was permissible to embrace them again. It was an outward manifestation of their choice to repent. No one should question or challenge the so-called 'man of God.' Doing so jeopardized one's salvation and life, as he frequently warned, "God will always choose the man of God over you."

A sick sense of entitlement developed within us, because we followed without question. Why? We were becoming 'Bride of Christ material' for dutifully standing with the 'man of God.'

You were significant, special: you became chosen.

The Point of No Return

I received permission to stay overnight with a friend from church. I thought this couple was unique. The Mom was charming and—within the limits of our clothing rules—fashionable. The dad was kind. It felt like I was in a rich home, with Little Debbie snacks of crème filling with a chocolate layer on the outside, and so many books. I will call this friend Tajana.

Looking back, I recognize that this friendship was part of my grooming. In my healing work, I've learned that predators often use other victims or enablers to introduce inappropriate content gradually.

She shared her love of music through her vinyl's, her library books, especially "Gone with the Wind." Being less than a year older than me made her even more intriguing. I finally found a close friend. I listened intently to everything she shared with me until one day she told me about oral sex.

What? It blew my mind. I had never heard of such things. This was so grotesque!

I couldn't understand how a 14-year-old knew about such things. We could not watch TV or movies. I learned about the scientific act of sex from James Dobson's book. It did not include this act. Sex was an act of love, but this sounded revolting to my 13-year-old mind. I was being educated, but I didn't understand why. What I now understand is that this premature sexual education was designed to normalize inappropriate sexual content. Her mom was the one who had pulled me aside at school because of my zeal, attracting attention. This was so bizarre. Did this family not follow the rules of being in 'the bride'?

Best friends can have so much influence in your life. Tajana had this power over me. I wanted to be like her. She was buying a birthday card for 'the man of God.' Terrific plan—I purchased one as well. I remember finding a card that was not frilly or silly. We would give him our cards to celebrate his early July birthday. She was 14 years old. I was 13 years old.

What seemed like a splendid idea turned my life around. There was no escape.

I was trapped. Someone turned the key.

I will never forget the sound of the lock clicking.

Next, I'll share how this innocent act of giving a birthday card became the doorway for years of abuse and manipulation. The seeds planted in these early days in the 'group' would grow into a nightmare I couldn't have imagined. But even in sharing these painful truths, I want you to know that healing is possible. My story doesn't end in that cage, and yours won't either.

I want to show you how to recognize these patterns before they trap you, and how to build genuine, healthy spiritual community. The journey ahead may be difficult to read as it was to live. You may need to take breaks, to breathe, to remind yourself that you are safe now. But I believe that by shining light in these dark places, we can help others recognize the warning signs before they hear their own cage door lock.

Red Flags: Warning Signs of the Manipulation System

I've identified these patterns of manipulation that appear in my story and often exist in religious environments where abuse occurs:

Elitism and exclusivity:
- Language of being "special," "elite," or "chosen"
- Terms like "bride member," "selection from a selection," "cream of the crop"
- Creating hierarchies within religious communities
- Emphasis on "deserving" special status through works or loyalty

Financial control:
- Requiring tithes before basic needs are met
- "Giving until it hurts" mentality
- Sacrificial giving that creates financial hardship
- Lack of support during financial difficulties

Surveillance and reporting:
- Having actions monitored and reported to leadership
- Restricted friendships and social activities
- Needing permission for normal activities
- "No outside friends" policies

Indoctrination techniques:
- Recordings played repeatedly in homes
- Public shaming through denouncing people in sermons
- Hours of listening to the same teacher/preacher
- Edited vs. "special" unedited materials

Restrictive rules around appearance:
- Strict, specific dress codes
- Monitoring of hairstyles and clothing
- Dress requirements that cause physical discomfort, impracticality, or unwanted disclosure
- Scrutiny of personal choices about appearance

Voice suppression:
- Controlling when and how you can express spiritual gifts
- Requiring permission for authentic expression
- Punishing genuine enthusiasm or spiritual fervor
- Making authentic voice dependent on approval

CHAPTER 4
The Trap

"Don't let the beauty mesmerize you. A gilded cage is still a cage. Paint it gold, put glowing lights on it and glimmering locks. It is still a prison." – Bridget

†

Through my healing work with survivors, I've learned that predators follow a precise grooming protocol. What I experienced wasn't random—it was a calculated sequence designed to trap and silence victims. Understanding this system is crucial for protection, because when you can see the pattern, you can interrupt it.

At thirteen, I walked directly into a trap that had been carefully prepared. What I'm about to share isn't just my story—it's a detailed case study in predatory grooming that I now use to educate families and communities about protection.

Let me show you exactly how it unfolded, so you can recognize these tactics before they ensnare you or someone you love.

Phase One: Creating Isolation and Opportunity

Predators understand that abuse requires opportunity. They systematically create situations where they can be alone with potential victims while maintaining plausible explanations for the isolation.

Tajana wasn't there with me to give the birthday card to Pastor Perseus. I was alone with him.

What I now recognize is that this isolation wasn't accidental. Behind the cracked door sat Pastor Perseus at his elegant, dark wood desk. I walked in with his birthday card. The dark wood-paneled walls surrounded me with books and art. It seemed like the office of an eloquent person. A safe place.

His wife wasn't there.

I was alone.

Predators carefully orchestrate these moments of isolation. Was this the plan all along? Was Tajana setting me up to include me in the scheme of the birthday card? What appears coincidental may have been calculated manipulation.

I walked right into the snare.

A thirteen-year-old should never be in the office of a man unaccompanied, but I didn't know this. Predators count on the fact that children naturally trust authority figures and don't recognize danger in 'safe' religious settings. It was my pastor, in his office, on the church premises, on a church service night.

My life was suddenly going to be changed forever.

What you can do now: Consider whether authority figures ever asked you to be alone with them without clear, supervised purposes. Remember that healthy leaders emphasize safety, transparency, and boundaries—not secrecy. Write what healthy leadership looks like to you. What specific questions can you ask to evaluate the safety protocols of religious organizations.

Phase Two: Trust Testing and Secret-Keeping

Predators always begin with trust testing. They need to know if their potential victim will maintain secrecy before they escalate to physical abuse.

I had never been alone in the Pastor's office before. He was no longer at his desk. Receiving my card, he was pleased. He hugged me. This wasn't a normal hug. I had never seen him hug a girl or a woman before.

He asked me, "Can I trust you?"

"Can you keep a secret and not tell anyone?"

He kept asking me the same thing. He was testing me.

What I now understand is that his trap was to make me feel special because he was a powerful leader. He wanted to take my voice. He wanted to see if I would be silent under the guise of holding a confidence. I didn't know that he wanted to see if I would stay in this cage that was opened. He was grooming me at that very moment, using trust to mislead me.

Predators use our natural desire to be trustworthy against us. I had confidence in this spiritual leader. My family moved across the nation to follow his leadership at the headquarters of his fellowship of churches. Other families left their churches to follow Pastor Perseus. He was the man of God, leading the special 'bride' called from the church to be the elite.

This birthday card was not permission for him to touch me.

He never told me the secret.

What we teach families in our prevention programs is that healthy leaders never ask children to keep secrets from their parents. Legitimate confidences are always age-appropriate and never involve physical contact or isolation.

Phase Three: Creating False Purpose and Escalating Access

Predators excel at creating legitimate-seeming reasons for increased access to their victims. This phase is designed to normalize regular private meetings while gradually escalating inappropriate behavior.

Obedience was the allegiance of every member that stayed in this church. What I now recognize is that this culture of unquestioning obedience created the perfect environment for abuse. The rules and standards of this group reflected this obedience. Many volunteered hours of their free time in loyalty to show their action of devotion as well.

I joined in my faithfulness by working in the church library. The church library was the catalyst for spreading the media of print and tapes to its many members. The church documented Pastor Perseus's messages for wider distribution.

When I was in his office with the birthday card, Pastor Perseus asked me to escape from the church library during the next week and come to his office. This was my first act of obedience designed to test my compliance. Maybe I was going to help him with something in his office? I was supposed to be going to the ladies' room. My journey of deception had begun.

We must address this critical question: the head librarian warned other girls who offered their time to never leave the library, under no circumstances. She didn't warn me. What I've learned through my prevention work is that some staff members knew danger existed but not all children were equally protected.

Some parents wouldn't let their daughters work in the church library. The head librarian did not caution me.

My hours of volunteering at the Church Library were really a free pass for harm that was damaging and life altering. What we now understand is that institutional knowledge of danger often exists without adequate protection measures. How many others escaped?

Phase Four: Crossing Physical Boundaries

This phase represents the predator's transition from grooming to assault. Understanding this progression helps survivors recognize that their confusion and inability to resist was a normal trauma response, not consent or failure.

He reached to kiss me on the lips. I was frozen and confused. Love is supposed to be wholesome. No one had ever kissed me like this.

I did not imagine my first kiss like that; it wasn't what I had dreamt of, and it wasn't consensual. Predators count on the fact that children have no framework for understanding inappropriate adult behavior. His authority commanded the blind obedience of many men and women. He preached behind the pulpit for many hours a week. He was writing books and sending out tapes of his sermons worldwide in the name of God, and he continually asked about my trustworthiness.

He had so much at risk. I could never share this with anyone. What I now understand is that this is exactly why predators target children in positions of trust and authority— the stakes make silence feel essential. His repeats turned into commands. I obeyed without question.

The gap in my heart was growing. This growing emptiness is a natural response to betrayal by trusted authority figures. Pastor Perseus swiftly put things in place so my family believed I was being counted on to help him in his office for secretary work beyond the volunteer work at the church library.

He presented interesting evidence of my needed services—folding letters and stuffing envelopes for mailers. It was an honor for their daughter to be chosen to work personally for him. Of course, no suspicions at all. Predators excel at creating cover stories that make parents feel proud rather than protective. My parents entrusted my services to him. I was helping the 'man of God.'

Pastor Perseus wanted to increase my visits for his own purposes. Initially, I may have worked, but gradually I left the envelopes in their boxes and never folded the letters.

These office visits during the week turned into abuse that escalated into rape. What we address in our healing workshops is the trauma of being trapped in situations where you desperately want to speak but cannot. My father would drop me off to help and I was screaming inside, "Please, Dad, don't drop me off! Don't make me go!" I was silent. No one could see my turmoil.

I had to hide it and never disclose it. My father loved this man, and his submission reflected his loyalty. This was his father in the Lord. Many, including my father, worshipped and idolized Pastor Perseus.

My molestation from Pastor Perseus was disguised in gentleness, but it is painful, disgusting and rough. The stench covered by his strong cologne, the white shirt, baggy trousers and polished black shoes are memories that only the cleansing blood of my Savior can erase.

I recall these to help you turn your memories over to Jesus. A healing balm for those ugly wounds and scars.

> **What you can do now:** Recognize that freezing is a normal trauma response. If you experienced abuse and couldn't fight or flee, this doesn't mean you consented or "let it happen." Write this truth: "My response to trauma was a normal survival mechanism, not a failure."

Phase Five: Spiritual Manipulation and Control

What I've learned through my prevention work is that religious predators weaponize faith itself to maintain control over their victims. This represents the most insidious form of spiritual abuse.

Pastor Perseus targeted me with spiritual manipulation. He would come up to me and my mother at church and make statements like, "If you wait, God will give you the very best." What I now recognize is that this was the foundation of his scheme—to keep me separate and alone using the name of God perversely about my future for his preservation.

This misuse of spiritual language serves multiple purposes: it isolates the victim from potential relationships while making the predator appear spiritually concerned for their welfare.

Each bar of my cage was named: Secrets. Lies. Shame. Bondage. Abuse. Innocence. The first steps toward freedom are survivors recognizing these 'bars'. Each represents a tool predators use to construct psychological cages around their victims.

> **What you can do now:** Consider the misuse of spiritual language to control and manipulate. For each 'bar' listed above, write a counter-truth (for example, counter 'Secrets' with 'I may speak my truth'). Replace these lies with liberating truths.

Phase Six: Systemic Failure and Multiple Predators

Abuse rarely occurs in isolation. When one predator operates freely, it often indicates systemic failures that enable multiple offenders.

This was a problem I encountered at the church school as well. What I now understand is that I wasn't guarded because the system itself was compromised. The Christian School I attended did not even offer me a haven of safety. The headteacher touched me. He molested me, never penetrating me.

I feared Pastor Perseus would find out. I didn't know how I was supposed to cope.

The more I was abused, the heavier my burden of silence became. Multiple traumas compound the isolation and confusion survivors experience. I dragged this weight every day and night. It reminded me of my vow of secrecy.

I lost weight. I was sickly. My body was keeping score. These physical symptoms are normal trauma responses that require professional support. This abuse afflicted my mind. I was living a hideous double life.

This blur of no questions asked overwhelmed me. Pastor Perseus started coming to the Christian School that was across town. This building was full of hidden rooms and dark passages. He stalked me here as well, telling me to meet him in a room. He held my head and forced me.

I couldn't escape these predators.

The staff let me roam these rooms unsupervised.

Others misrepresented my safe environment. Predators depend on their victims maintaining normal appearances while suffering privately. My schoolmates who were my friends surrounded me. I testified and enjoyed worship in the chapel services at the church school. This was supposed to be a joyous time for me, being part of the 'special church,' playing my trumpet in the church band.

Now I was part of the 'private circle,' the 'selected ones,' but it was just a torturous dream I couldn't awake from.

The questions haunted me: What was the purpose of me even being alive? Was my existence a mistake? Did I deserve this? Where was the authentic Bridget?

I couldn't escape these questions.

Mentally I spiraled. I almost told my mom. I wanted to share all of my burdens with her. This moment represents the survivor's inner wisdom trying to break through. My breaking point had arrived. My memory of it is clear; it happened in the kitchen. I could not say it. I was speechless. These abusive men took my voice.

If only I would have been brave enough, despite the consequences.

The questions I couldn't answer: Would she have believed me? Why didn't I yell stop? Why was I never warned to never be in a room alone with a man? Why weren't safety measures put in place for clergy members and church staff? How long had this ministry tolerated this behavior?

Breaking the Cycle: From Victim to Victor

What transformed my understanding was learning that I wasn't alone—and that my voice could prevent other children from experiencing what I did.

The headteacher's sexual assaults suddenly stopped after a brief period. What I later learned was that the headteacher found out that Pastor Perseus had secretly captured me for himself. Later on, I would learn that girls were not safe around Pastor Perseus or the headteacher.

The headteacher of the church school had also been molesting the girls in the school, and one witness told me she was raped after he molested her for a time. No one ever stopped him.

Pastor Perseus had left a trail of victims before me. When I came out with my story, I learned I was one of many. This pattern of abuse was happening before I moved—and would have continued after I left without intervention.

One victim reported to me she knew I was Pastor Perseus' replacement. She escaped him by graduating from school and getting married. However, he taunted her and targeted her with actions in front of others to humiliate her. I never knew this before.

Therefore, I'm writing my story to break up and demolish these silent clubs of shame and abuse. We must join hands as victors, not victims. We must speak, even if it is just a whisper. "I have survived, and I will thrive again!"

Safety measures need to be taken in all institutions of children and young people, especially a Christian School. We will stop this cycle of freedom to manipulate and brainwash.

This charismatic man, called a pastor, 'God's man,' manipulated women and young girls. I was becoming the next statistic. Instead of alerting me, they silently welcomed me into the circle of those abused and victimized. What our prevention work addresses is how institutions can become complicit through silence and inaction.

This twisted paradigm survived through collective silence and institutional failure.

By my fourteenth birthday, Pastor Perseus was sneaking through the back door of our house, which was down the street from the church. He was making a bold step blinded by his thirst for sin. My parents were unaware. I was so terrified that they would come home and find that he was forcing himself on me there, right in the living room. Again, I could not escape. I was anguished and sickened.

My heart was hemorrhaging. I was muted.

No one would believe a fourteen-year-old.

This was not my fault.

But, even in the darkest moments, I clung to the truth that there was light beyond this cage. I tried to capture this in a poem.

The Shadows

In the shadows lurks my biggest fears and doubts,
Memories that are just as dark finds a place in the
hedge of guilt and sorrow.
I must stay close to the Shepherd.
He knows this snarly, ugly hedge that looms around
my soul.
He will protect me.
I must stay close to Him.
I dwell in His shadow, the Cross, my redemption and
rescue.
He has forgiven me.
I belong to Him, I rejoice as I huddle close to Him
and I rest, safe and secure.

—Bridget Goodwin, 2021

Because this darkness needs to be called out, I'll share how this abuse continued through my teenage years, and the growing isolation that made escape seem impossible. Despite my inner world collapsing, others pressured me to maintain a perfect appearance of holiness and submission.

The journey through this darkness may be difficult to read, but I share it because I know many of you have walked similar paths. The shame that kept me silent for decades is the same shame that may be keeping you silent now. But there is hope beyond the shadows—a light that can penetrate even the darkest cage.

What I've learned through my healing work is that breaking silence is the first step toward freedom—both for survivors and for preventing future abuse. Stay with me. Your healing journey matters, and together we can break the silence that protects abusers and imprisons survivors.

CHAPTER 5
The Scheme, the Plan, the Plot

"Love will survive the storms of life, not the house of cards built on propaganda." – Bridget

†

What you're about to read reveals the sophisticated machinery of spiritual abuse—the systematic methods predators use to maintain long-term control. These aren't random acts of manipulation, but calculated strategies designed to trap victims in webs of false spirituality and manufactured dependency. As someone who survived fifteen years in this system and now guides other survivors through healing, I can show you exactly how these schemes operate—and more importantly, how to recognize and escape them.

The molesting and pedophilia couldn't continue without a scheme. Someone had to create a plan to maintain the abuse, to keep it hidden, to make it sustainable over years.

At fifteen, I was isolated by design. Boys were pursuing me, my friends were having boyfriends, but this normal teenage experience was exactly what made me dangerous to control. They could influence me and challenge my lifestyle. So I was kept isolated. Dominated. The typical enjoyment of a teenager became out of the question.

And then Pastor Perseus revealed his plan.

His wife would die, he told me, and one day I would be his wife. This was supposedly a revelation from God—a false prophetic word. I was to wait, pray, and plan for this future. Save myself for him and my divine destiny.

This was evil, to pray for someone to die!

This false prophecy pattern—it always involves isolation and waiting for something that will never come. This was the secret, the twisted plot all along.

Walking to his office at church from my house was becoming risky. Pastor Perseus needed to come to my home, but this wouldn't work without my parents in agreement.

I couldn't tell my brother.

We shared a lovely relationship as brother and sister growing up. The roles changed as we grew older—no longer me mothering him, but me leaning on him to feel safe. He was a dare-devil, and I was the cautious one. Here I was, scared, but not cautious. My situation trapped, silenced, and stunned me as I held this ugly secret from him.

It brings me great sadness that I didn't scream, whisper, or tell my brother.

Expanding the Web of Control

Pastor Perseus planted an idea, a seed. Your daughter was going to have an outstanding future. He cultivated and grew this false prophecy. I lost my identity. He chose my clothing, creating me into the wife-to-be. He purchased a 'hope' chest for me to store treasures for my new life that was going to happen. Not to a young man, but to a married man, because one day soon his wife was going to die.

He replaced my cardboard boxes with furniture that he bought for me. He chose a piano for me, supposedly from my father, when actually Perseus gave the monthly payments to my father and mother. I chose none of these items. He continued to shower me with expensive gifts.

Of course, my parents allowed this 'man of God' into their home. Their daughter was receiving preferential treatment. The brainwashing and programming were working. But this wasn't the typical love story of dating, of being adored and celebrated. This was domination. My life was being pulled out of me, my purity forever gone. This wasn't how a bride should prepare for the most glorious day of her life, her wedding.

Perseus set the frame of the house of cards in place. The gifts were only bribes to keep me silent. He was grooming not only me but my parents. I was now a prisoner in my home and in my own room.

I want you to recognize these manipulation tactics as they unfolded in my story. Perseus used future-faking—making impossible promises about his wife dying and creating a 'divine destiny' narrative. He used spiritual language to justify my waiting, keeping me in limbo with vague timelines, manipulating my life decisions through false prophecy.

He manipulated my entire family—including my parents in the grooming process, providing financial benefits, creating illusions of favor and blessing, gradually taking control of family decisions. My family members became tools to monitor and control me.

The social isolation was systematic. He prevented normal peer relationships, blocked any college or educational opportunities, restricted friendships, monitored and limited family connections. Specifically blocking education for females enforced strict gender roles that limited my options.

He created complete dependency. He controlled my transportation—not allowing me to drive. He managed finances and purchasing decisions, made decisions about our living arrangements, paid for our vacations to maintain control, regulated when and where I could travel. Every privilege felt like his special concession.

Perseus cultivated a false sense of specialness—I was part of a 'special circle,' had a unique 'divine' future, was singled out as different from my peers. He created a counterfeit identity and purpose, groomed me to accept an artificial role, made every decision supposedly 'for my own good.'

The elaborate deception required complex lies to mask his behavior. Moving our house helped him better hide his misconduct. He involved others in maintaining secrecy, built a facade that appeared legitimate, enlisted multiple people in the deception, created cover stories for suspicious behavior.

This long-term control maintained itself over decades. He incrementally increased freedoms as 'rewards,' created a false normal that I accepted, used his vasectomy to prevent pregnancy evidence, taught me to self-police my behavior, made me feel grateful for small freedoms.

The signs of predatory intent were everywhere. His vasectomy prevented evidence of sexual activity. He preemptively addressed potential accusations, used his position of authority to silence questions, maintained multiple victims in rotation, planned for long-term access to victims, created systems of mutual silence among victims.

My parents couldn't have close friends. We had to keep our California friends at arm's length. One day, Perseus found out we were at their house, enjoying sweet fellowship. I believe he drove by spying on us. He put a stop to it.

Otherwise, this might have become a topic of discussion— my parents' secrecy, Perseus visiting their underage daughter in their home. The whisper of friends heard by my parents might have blown down this house of cards. The collapse would have been liberating. Friends who love you ask the right questions to protect you. The words may sting, but they slap you into reality.

If only my parents had heard from them, "This isn't normal. Save your daughter and your family."

I'm sure Perseus questioned my parents' trustworthiness.

My parents accepted the investment into my future. This takeover of my life damaged my soul. I learned to accept my dilemma as it turned into a daydream.

Perseus had no right to take the place of Jesus Christ. No one using this title 'man of God' should take power over an individual, family, or church. The church belongs to Jesus. Our Savior Jesus came to rescue, save, and redeem. The name of Jesus should never promote fear or support prophecy that allows sin and evil to be cultivated.

We must stop this!

If these patterns feel familiar, my free guide 'Recognizing Spiritual Manipulation' can help you identify them in any religious setting. You can download it at ihaveavoice.love.

What you can do now: Consider how manipulators might use gifts, financial support, or "special treatment" as control tools. Make a list of any concerning patterns of control in your family relationships. Remember that healthy love supports autonomy rather than creating dependency.

Keeping Victims Ignorant and Dependent

I wanted to escape the church school and its headteacher. As a tenth-grader, my hard work had earned me early graduation credits at only 15 years old, but they were still controlling my future. Girls couldn't go to college or university—this was part of the rules of the 'group.' The group preached that a young woman's role was to marry and have children.

Education would have liberated me. Knowledge would have shaped my perspective, developed my ability to question, to challenge wrongs—even these sins that society agrees are immoral. How puzzling that a place of God would feed me such warped truths?

I had two things working against me: I was a woman, and I lived in isolation. Education is vital for all girls to be safe!

My place was to be isolated and wait. Surely my day would come. Perseus coerced me to believe this was from God, but God doesn't promote or prophesy sin in one's life. Sin is sin, no exception to the rule. Perseus obscured my understanding of God's living Word. I was in darkness. Any church—any system or group of people who practice excessive devotion to a figure, object, or belief system, typically following a charismatic leader—is a cult.

I was in a cult.

"I was in a cult"—often becomes the first breakthrough moment for survivors. I had accepted my destiny without question.

When the Mask Began to Slip

My parents may have given permission for weekly visits in our home, but they remained oblivious to the debauchery happening behind my locked bedroom door. This wicked vice had become my normal. This man was to be my husband one day, so I saved myself for him and our future. I was faithful to a fault.

I couldn't escape.

Then Perseus got careless. Someone saw his shiny Cadillac in our driveway a few streets from the church. He'd delivered flowers himself, and someone noticed. Gifts were being seen. Church office staff started asking questions.

A rumble started, so Perseus created a scheme. My mom would lie and say the flowers were for her because she'd been ill. Anything built on lies is wrong. God detests lies and falsehoods. This 'man of God' now had others being dishonest for him. Incredibly, he made these declarations during a church service to establish the falsehoods! Even the office staff were involved in lying to protect Perseus' sin.

Even good people can be 'brainwashed' to lie to protect the agenda of a so-called 'man of God.' My mother wasn't the only one who had to lie to protect this wicked prophecy, this evil plan that involved my life and future. Perseus used this as his license to sin, grooming and manipulating anyone who sensed something was wrong.

Others have shared with me later that they knew something was wrong, but who would believe them if they spoke up? Some told me they were sorry for not saying something to stop it. Even they were silenced.

This collective silence appears in every case of systematic church abuse I've encountered through my work with other survivors.

This man, Perseus, had too much power.

What you can do now: Pay attention to the power of collective silence. If you notice others making excuses or creating cover stories for someone in authority, this may reveal a broader pattern of deception. Consider what it might mean to be one voice that breaks the silence, even when it feels risky.

Controlling Every Aspect of Life

As the rumors grew louder, Perseus needed even tighter control over the environment where his abuse could continue undetected.

To keep the ruse going, we had to move so Perseus could park in a garage for his frequent visits during the week. To keep the involvement secret, he gave my parents money to make the move. My parents were so deceived that they weren't aware of what was happening behind my locked bedroom door. I was being choked, unaware that I was being confined.

My whole family was now controlled and manipulated.

The False Bride

I dreamed and planned. I looked at Bride Magazines with anticipation. My uniqueness became a false fantasy. A fabricated future was mine. My wedding plans filled me with excitement. I thought that I was in control of the planning. I believed this was God's will for my life.

I couldn't see that this married 'man of God' who consumed my life was pushing me toward hell. Torment and misery in my life came from hiding this life of sin.

This wasn't love!

I thought it was.

The sadness of those years—the waiting, the loneliness, the false hope—stays with me even now. I tried to capture those feelings in the next poem.

My Sad Ballad

My notes are sad today, blue tones of loneliness.
Dreams of the night haunt me with past memories.
I try to rise forth in these episodes of my dreams, my
voice no longer silent, but speaking the alarms of warning.
I'm shocked in my dreams by those who stand, those
who have suffered along with me.
These blue notes ring from my sad soul, sad because
I have waited so long to sing my song.
I'm blue, so very sad to relive this, to realize the
depravity of it all.

— Bridget Goodwin, 2021

I was 16, waiting. Seventeen came and went. I was 18, an adult, but now chained more than ever to this man. No freedom. I wasn't even allowed to drive. Yet I accepted this. The cost of what I thought was love and submission governed me. I longed to run away. I would fantasize about it, calling a cab to come and get me.

Would Perseus come and find me? Would he destroy my character?

Vacations away with my family were an escape for me. These times were a comfort. No hiding, no pretending, just fun and laughter, living life as it should be. I would long to postpone my return and, sometimes, I could convince Perseus to let me stay away longer. He even regulated my trips. He thought he had the right because he paid for them. I couldn't go alone, so he sponsored my parents as well.

What you can do now: Identify any areas where you've been living a "counterfeit" version of your life to please others. Write one authentic desire or dream you have for yourself. Taking small steps toward genuine self-expression can counter years of false identity.

Stolen Years

This house of cards was teetering. They included others in 'the special circle,' a web of deception—a facade propped against the leaning structure. It became more apparent to them that I was the substitute wife. This limited number of people in the church knew I was preserving myself for Perseus. They weren't aware that this abuse started when I was 13 years old, that their pastor had targeted a minor.

I was 19, 20, 21, 22—still waiting for 'God's best.' I watched my friends get married one by one. My heart would break and I would just weep that it wasn't me.

How long did I have to wait? My loyalty and devotion were absolute. I hadn't realized that my voice had become his voice. I didn't realize I could escape my cage; instead, I decorated it and made it comfortable.

This shouldn't have been acceptable.

I was 23, 24, 25, 26. The grip of control eased slightly. I was allowed to have a car! By now, I had earned his trust. Yet Perseus put boundaries in place. Curfews were in order. I had no issues—I was used to obeying. He struggled with the decision to let me drive. I fought for this to happen. I won. My elation was immense!

At 27, 28—I bought a wedding dress. How this web had entangled me. Those who were around me, who knew or had suspicions—why didn't they kill the spider? I carried out all my plans in isolation.

No banners that read, "I Found the Dress!" No celebratory toasts.

I was going into this with one certainty: I would never be a mother and hold my child in my arms. Perseus had gotten a vasectomy years before me so no one could claim he was the father of their child. Because of this—thankfully—I never became pregnant. But why would a man, let alone a 'man of God,' even make such a claim unless he was promiscuous? And why would he say this from the pulpit to his congregation that had him on a worshipped pedestal?

If you recognize these patterns in your current church or religious community, you're not alone, and it's not your fault.

I journeyed through the dark years of captivity, and they may be difficult to read. But I am going to share these details with you next because I know many survivors have lost significant portions of their lives in abusive situations. Know that you are not alone in feeling that precious years were stolen from you, and it's never too late to reclaim your authentic self and create a life of genuine meaning.

Even as for me, as I bought a wedding dress at 28 years old, forces were already in motion that would eventually set me free—though freedom would come with its own painful path.

In the next chapter, I'll share how this fifteen-year old nightmare finally unraveled.

CHAPTER 6
Freedom Begins

"A bird was created to fly. The sky is its home. Put it in a cage. You have sentenced it to death. Just like love, it is liberating, not controlling, it needs to be set free to fly." – Bridget

†

The systematic manipulation tactics religious predators use to maintain control are a carefully orchestrated pattern. What happened to me wasn't unique.

The leadership of my church used terror, bullying, and fabricated rules outside of God's Word to maintain intense control over their members. Pastor Perseus twisted scripture under the guise of biblical authority, promoting "lying to protect the man of God." He'd preach about Rahab from the book of Joshua—the woman who hid the Israelite spies and lied to protect them from the king of Jericho. Perseus convinced everyone it was acceptable to lie to protect "God's people," especially leadership.

Yet lying to protect evil and sin is never acceptable. Leadership should never use their power to influence those in their ministerial care to sin against God. Perseus blasphemously twisted great Bible stories to fit his corrupt narrative. Those who didn't follow his rules faced public humiliation from the pulpit. Fear of consequences kept everyone in line, creating blind followers.

This systematic approach to spiritual abuse included establishing informer networks that played on his congregation's vulnerabilities. He knew exactly which members would "lie and protect him." This environment enabled his and others' debauchery—extreme indulgence in bodily pleasures, especially sexual pleasures. This sexual abuse continued for decades, with multiple victims.

How do I know this? When I shared my story, several others confidentially came forward as victims too—of both Pastor Perseus and the headteacher.

Why did people look away? Several told me they regretted not speaking up to stop it, but their fear of opposing the cult leader silenced them. Who would've believed them?

We must unmask and halt all evil VIPs. Organizations need safety measures to recognize these red flags, with clear reporting procedures that are discussed and practiced. This creates a safe place for all ages. NO ONE should be exempt from the reporting process. We can stop brainwashing through awareness and established alert systems.

The VIP Factor

While there are many reasons victims don't tell, the VIP Factor is a significant reason sexual crimes against children have continued for generations. These Very Important Persons are well-known local leaders in our schools, athletic and civic organizations, houses of worship, healthcare and business communities. Some hold power at the state or national level—in education, law, military, corporate, media, higher education, and politics. They have power and money, and they've imposed a culture of silence that few dare attempt to confront.

The pulpit became Perseus' command center, where his words established a diabolical order. No gossip allowed. No "cliques." No families getting close. Attend all church activities. Plan vacations around church meetings across the USA. Volunteer free time several nights each week. He even micromanaged family time, keeping members entangled in his brainwashing.

Leading churches throughout the USA and worldwide, Perseus spoke for hours at every event as the keynote speaker. Young and old alike sought his approval at these meetings. He used his pulpit power to push his agenda, which proved essential for maintaining his labyrinth of dishonesty and his continued involvement in my life—covering up his evil and ungodly behavior.

It sickens me that he twisted God's sacred Word to sustain his sinful life.

These tactics formed the unholy chains that kept me shackled to my abuser into adulthood. I had been deceived and brainwashed. My entire future rested on lies and sin. My parents, the entire congregation, and I followed blindly. Making independent decisions terrified us, so we stayed, never questioning.

Even bystanders couldn't help being affected and contaminated. The silence became the loudest approval, transforming us into robotic, emotionless followers of this "man of God." He rewarded us with an immense sense of empowerment when we became the 'special called' ones who never questioned authority but would 'lie to protect.'

We believed this reward was special because he twisted 'the prophet's reward' from Jesus' teaching in Matthew 10:40-42. Jesus spoke about giving even a cup of cold water to a disciple—about the reward that comes from simple acts of service and kindness. But you should never isolate scripture to validate an agenda. Read the surrounding verses and chapters. What's the overall message? This passage speaks about the reward of accepting Jesus and His Father. Those who work alongside to establish Jesus' name through discipleship will receive rewards. We start with minor acts of service—the smallest act of giving and receiving.

This teaches about giving, not covering up evil.

Evil will never be rewarded.

This wasn't just sexual abuse—it was church abuse.

Recognizing Church Abuse vs. Healthy Faith

Three key characteristics of church abuse.

First, when the church tries to replace Jesus in your life, that's abuse.

The church should point you toward Jesus through life's difficulties, with congregants helping bear your burdens. Scripture tells us in Galatians 6:2 to *"bear one another's burdens."* God's Word nurtures your soul, drawing you to the promises of eternal life, Jesus' presence, and our Heavenly Father's endless care.

Abusive churches declare that listening to the 'man of God' means listening to Christ himself—that their leader is God's mouthpiece. They structure the order as Christ, then the 'man of God,' then man, and finally the woman. Yet scripture is clear in Colossians 1:18: *"And he is the head of the body, the church." Only Jesus deserves this powerful position as the "image of the invisible God, the firstborn of all creation. For by him all things were created, in heaven and on earth, visible and invisible, whether thrones or dominions or rulers or authorities—all things were created through him and for him."* (Colossians 1:15-16)

No man should ever stand in God's place! If you're in a church that positions leadership this way, leave!

Second, an abusive church keeps its congregants separated to prevent genuine community.

Leadership stunts genuine community, discouraging members from sharing life's trials. We called each other 'brother and sister,' but we functioned as a dysfunctional family full of secrets.

To truly bear another's burdens, you must walk alongside them, sharing their struggles. Pray together; seek God's direction together. We rarely spent time with other congregants outside church functions. True growth fulfills God's commission to *"bear one another's burdens."* You weren't meant to carry life's burdens alone.

Find your community, your people, God's church—a place to grow in following Him, an environment to develop your gifts.

Third, it's all about control—every aspect of your life: family, free time, relationships, finances, and dress.

This church abuse hemorrhages your heart into sworn allegiance—blood drop by blood drop—to a religious system centered on a man instead of Jesus. This isn't Christ's beloved church awaiting His return. We're not required to give our blood; He shed His blood for us on the cross.

His true church walks beside Him, listening to His voice, dedicating themselves to serving His kingdom on earth, sharing redemption, grace, and freedom. That's it—serving Jesus brings freedom, not religious mindsets.

The Holy Spirit gives us power to overcome our weaknesses and put on Christ instead of our sinful nature. We bear fruit because our lives aren't dead but alive in Jesus—we become like Him, *"filled with the fruit of righteousness that comes through Jesus Christ, to the glory and praise of God."* (Philippians 1:11)

This freedom liberates us, because *"where the Spirit of the Lord is, there is freedom."* (2 Corinthians 3:17) The result: *"the fruit of the Spirit...love, joy, peace, patience, kindness, goodness, faithfulness."* (Galatians 5:22)

This is exciting—a church full of life and vibrancy! Congregants lean on each other, gaining strength for daily life and its struggles. Leadership continually points everyone to God's Spirit, who gives love and self-control.

We make commitments to Jesus that affect our daily walk because we love Him. We receive scripture and sermons from leadership that remind us of God's Word's beautiful promises.

This is a healthy church! Jesus stands at the center—why? Because He embodies all power, strength, and beauty. He gave His life for us, the church, His people, His beloved.

What you can do now: Create a personal 'church health checklist' based on these three warning signs. For each point, write what a healthy spiritual community looks like in contrast. Use this to evaluate your current or future church environments. Our workshops provide guided exercises and community support for safely evaluating spiritual communities and rebuilding healthy faith.

Recognizing Dangerous Church Culture

The church abuse created room for sexual abuse. Giving such power and allegiance to one man proved detrimental. Churches need accountability boards that hold leadership responsible. Protecting, loving, and restoring the vulnerable—not preying on them—should be the church's main ethos. The church represents Jesus, who said: *"Come to me, all who labour and are heavy laden, and I will give you rest."* (Matthew 11:28)

Rest stands opposite to feeling unsafe.

Living in fear marks cult involvement.

This cultish church envisioned a 'selection from the church' they called the 'bride'—a 'selection from a selection'—where only a few received the 'special calling.' Terror was created through exclusion rather than inclusion. His Bride is the Church; this is the truth, contrary to past teaching. We eagerly await Jesus' return, our heavenly groom!

"Let us rejoice and exult and give him the glory, for the marriage of the Lamb (Jesus) has come, and his Bride has made herself ready; and it was granted her to clothe herself with fine linen, bright and pure—for the fine linen is the righteous deed of the saints." (Revelation 19:7-8)

We're created with a deep need to belong, to feel special, and our hearts belong to our Creator. We long for community, a tribe, people to commune with.

A cult doesn't cultivate healthy relationships.

The signs were everywhere, though I couldn't see them then. Cults isolate members and penalize them for leaving. They seek inappropriate loyalty to their leaders while dishonoring the family unit. They establish absolute authoritarianism without meaningful accountability.

There's no tolerance for questions or critical inquiry, no meaningful financial disclosure regarding budget or expenses—no independently audited financial statements. They create unreasonable fear about the outside world: impending catastrophe, evil conspiracies, persecutions. There's no legitimate reason to leave; former followers are always wrong in leaving, negative or even evil. Followers feel they can never be 'good enough.'

The group and its leader are always right. The leader becomes the exclusive means of knowing 'truth' or receiving validation; no other process of discovery is acceptable or credible.

Our church checked every one of these boxes.

Red Flags: Your Safety Checklist

• **Scripture Twisting** – Using biblical stories out of context to justify wrongdoing, applying scripture selectively to maintain control, creating 'special' interpretations of well-known passages, using God's name to intimidate and silence questions

• **Informant Networks** – Creating systems where members report on each other, using surveillance to maintain control, encouraging members to monitor 'suspicious' behavior, creating an atmosphere of constant observation

• **Institutional Protection of Abusers** – Multiple victims across long periods of time, patterns of abuse known but ignored, silence as institutional policy, attacking those who speak up rather than addressing reports

• **Cult-Like Environment** – Exclusive 'special' language and identity, unreasonable demands on time and resources, total control of relationships and activities, no tolerance for questioning or critical thinking, leader seen as beyond accountability

• **Stockholm Syndrome Indicators** – Developing emotional attachment to an abuser, interpreting control and abuse as care and love, difficulty separating even after physical freedom, grieving the loss of the abuser despite harm caused

When Control Systems Begin to Crack

Eventually, church members began talking because things weren't right. Bystanders noticed what was happening. Questions about authority abuse arose: 'Are immoral things happening?' Reports and rumors spread; unrest grew. People questioned the church's direction under this one man. Pastor Perseus tried maintaining control through preaching ultimatums.

The IRS scrutinized Pastor Perseus for tax evasion.

A wounded church member created a website reporting Pastor Perseus' and the Head Teacher's past sexual affairs. She revealed her sister's abuse and affair with Pastor Perseus. This website evolved into a massive forum where wounded current and former members could speak out.

Pastor Perseus told us she was lying and declared that "if she didn't die the death of all women, then he wasn't a man of God." Some even prayed for her death, brainwashed into believing the man of God was untouchable and blameless. This evil response further harmed wounded members, who faced excommunication instead of receiving help.

The church grew deeply unsettled, tossing like a boat in a storm. Too many circumstances were arising; things weren't adding up!

Pastor Perseus made more declarations in his church messages, attempting to keep the rocking ship from imploding. "If God has deceived me and is through with my ministry, He needs to just take me." During another service, he declared: "God didn't stand a seducing spirit up here! He stood a 'power of the world to come' behind this pulpit! Someone to be respected!"

These were threats, and God heard them along with the people. God isn't mocked. These weren't innocent responses. Humility and grace should characterize a man following God and leading His entrusted sheep. This was a wolf in sheep's clothing.

Then it happened.

Suddenly, on Saturday night, July 20th, he preached for an hour and a half, then sat down. Within minutes, he stood up, left the platform, and suffered a massive heart attack on the back steps.

He died.

What you can do now: If you're observing concerning behaviors in a religious organization or any group, document them with specific dates and details. Research safe reporting options outside the organization and consider contacting professionals who specialize in helping those leaving high-control groups.

Processing Unexpected Freedom

The church never expected this. He'd proclaimed 'prophecies' and 'divine encounters' that were clearly false. It became increasingly evident that his 'prophecies,' both public and private, weren't true.

God isn't mocked. No one escapes accountability.

It ended.

I was 28 years old; Perseus died at 63.

I screamed, yelled, sobbed—how could this happen? I had waited 16 years. I couldn't believe he was dead. I rushed to the hospital. Yes, he had died, the breathing tube still in his mouth.

I walked away, stunned, in a dream-like state. He'd made me so many promises, all now revealed as lies. I felt broken, angry, hurt, lost, and grief-stricken. The spell of false love began disintegrating with every tear I shed. The tears became my reality check, starting my path to liberation!

Crowds gathered for Perseus' funeral; his body lay in the church sanctuary for viewing several days. They kept him on display to accommodate worldwide travelers paying respects. It seemed strange how crisis united people when evil had previously reigned. The disgruntled remained silent during this mourning period. Perseus' hold continued even after death. Others feared being wrong; it wasn't time to bravely speak out that his death wasn't coincidental. His own words had come to pass: "If God is done with me, He should just take me."

Everything blurred into mourning black with the overbearing aroma of countless flowers. They displayed him in church for days like a hero deserving respectful mourning. His sinful life ended the day he died.

I said my goodbyes at his casket. Though free, I stayed with these people and grieved. I didn't realize I could've run far away. I felt so broken I couldn't find my voice. My shoulders hunched beneath years of chains to this false dream, lies, shame, and guilt.

The chains had gone; he was dead, yet I still couldn't stand straight.

I visited his grave almost daily—where else could I go?

I grieved intensely, contemplating my life, which seemed over. How could I ever love again? How would I cope? I felt so alone and afraid.

I raged.

I screamed.

I wept uncontrollably.

My dad grew so concerned he hid my handgun.

I searched for a glimmer of hope. So many wasted years bearing guilt, hiding, praying for something awful—the evil hope that his wife would die so I could marry Perseus. I'd been deceived into believing this was God's calling for me. Now I faced it alone.

He died, leaving his widow to handle the aftermath. She went on to live a liberated life—traveling worldwide, buying a car, learning to drive. For a time, she moved to Africa and truly lived. Freedom, too, was found by her. Who knows what she knew? She knew about me, but maybe not the entire story—or perhaps she did. I'll never know. Twenty-two years after her husband's death, she died. God isn't mocked; she lived long and wonderfully. Perhaps her later years proved best.

Taking Your First Steps Toward a New Life

A month later came my birthday. My father had flowers delivered to my workplace. He found freedom too. The rift between us began healing. He showed me such love and kindness during this period.

I made my first brave step—shutting the door on my past. I needed to continue. I wanted to leave my old life behind and start fresh.

This became my moment of truth. A dear man who later became my father-in-law asked what I would do now. I had made my bed and must lie in it. Yes, I suffered in agony because I'd allowed deceit to control my life, but now I could decide my next step.

Time to find my voice!

Throughout everything, I clung to God. I prayed and started journaling after Perseus' death, recording my feelings to process grief and navigate the following weeks. I knew I needed to close my journal, stop writing about Perseus, and move forward. No more reflection—just my voice, my life, my future, my time to run toward it! This poem reflects that Jesus can take the burden for me, and help me leave the weight of the memories behind me.

My Burden

Today I realized as I went for prayer that I'm better,
but deep down I'm still grieving.
I can go to Jesus to take this burden.
This lock of this secret of 40 years has been broken.
The more I talk and share, the lighter this burden feels.
This burden is like a backpack on my back,
Each event, each memory must go,
Rocks and boulders, one by one,
Pulled out of this burden strapped on my back.
This is what Jesus is doing in my life, bestowing grace
and truth, to relieve me of this burden.
Grace to forgive and truth to replace the lies and
deception.
May I lay aside every stone, and run this race,
keeping the pace set by my Savior.
His yoke is easy, His burden is light.

—Bridget Goodwin, 2021

Discovering True Freedom and Authentic Love

I'd been caged so long I didn't even realize this was my Independence Day—the day Perseus died.

I'd lived over half my life waiting, submitting, planning, and loving the man I thought would be my future husband.

What I didn't realize then was that I'd been living with Stockholm Syndrome—a condition where hostages develop strong psychological bonds with their captors as a survival strategy during captivity. These feelings result from intimate time spent together. It's considered irrational given the danger and risk experienced by victims. The danger of someone discovering Perseus' sexual involvement in my life and the risk of being seen together vanished. The physical bond broke. Though I hadn't realized it yet—I'd been set free!

Just like dawn breaking after a stormy night, vibrant light pierced my long darkness. Someone entered my heart: Jonathan.

This felt exhilarating—and it was my choice. I pursued him. I'd known him since childhood as my brother's best friend. I was a few years older, but I didn't have time to waste.

Jonathan contrasted completely with the manipulative, threatening, suffocating, coercive man who had controlled 16 years of my life. Jonathan showed kindness, spoke softly, behaved gently, made me laugh, and demonstrated thoughtfulness. I teach in my workshops that any relationship involving manipulation, control, and gaslighting isn't love—it's abuse.

Almost two months later, I called Jonathan but hung up before he answered. I felt scared.

Could I start over?

Could I experience a delightful future?

Did I have a chance or did I already ruin the moment?

A week later I called again but didn't hang up. We talked for nearly an hour. This felt so different—sweet, fun, innocent. My heart soared; I felt giddy, excited, seeing light break through my darkness.

We began dating. How thrilling to eat together without hiding! Pizza, nachos, caramel malt shakes, expensive and inexpensive meals—all tasted like exquisite castle dining hall feasts.

This wasn't fantasy—this was real love. I detoxed from false love's poison. Every distorted memory gave way to good, wholesome, exciting love.

Jonathan taught me what love could be, and I wanted it more than anything. I longed to spend my life with him. I learned I could love again, this time without force. This wasn't the 'captor and captive' Stockholm Syndrome relationship. This love liberated me—my heart wanted to fly and dance.

What you can do now: Identify three small but meaningful decisions you can make for yourself this coming week. These might be as simple as choosing what to eat, what to wear, or how to spend your free time. Practice making choices without seeking permission or approval from others.

Releasing the Past's Hold

It was time for a fresh start. I destroyed, burned, cut up, and discarded all correspondence, tapes, and pictures from Perseus.

Jonathan didn't know about my abusive past that began when I was 13.

I wouldn't reopen that door; I'd closed it. I turned away from it to start over—this time by my choice. Unknown to me, others advised Jonathan not to ask about my past. The culture of lying to cover leadership's sins affected him too. Questions emerged years later. The blind obedience teaching suppressed the truth in our relationship. Only God preserved our budding love when I finally answered all his questions years later.

I wanted to marry Jonathan without a long wait. Our love grew, and I knew he was right for me. Now that I could choose, my parents questioned everything I did. The spell had broken. My parents had found freedom too. They asked questions, but I told them this differed from before. This represented my future and my choice. Jonathan's parents supported us. Five months later we married, and my life filled with hope for my future with my true love, Johnny.

Building a New Life Beyond the High-Control Environment

After Perseus died, the church began splintering. The strong cult leader had gone, and people felt free to leave. Over three-quarters of the church departed—some searching for another strong leader, others simply quitting from weariness. The few remaining became more loyal, trying to salvage what remained. Leadership struggled to maintain control. My family left, moving south to find new spiritual leadership. This tore my family apart, but I clung to my new husband.

Despite the church upheaval, I focused on my new life. My musical career took off with Jonathan's encouragement to spread my wings and live the American dream. I opened a music store with an instrument storefront and teaching studio.

Love cultivates dreams and creates space for them to grow in relationships. Our love's blessings showed as our store expanded—a year later, we moved to a larger location.

Our love produced a dream come true. After months of waiting and worrying, I became pregnant. I had a blue-eyed, blonde-haired little boy. We named him Samuel, 'gift of God.' Twenty-two months later came another blessing—a brown-eyed, brown-haired boy. We named him Josiah, 'whom Jehovah heals.'

God's blessings overwhelmed me despite my church turmoil. God worked in our home, marriage, family, and business. Life challenged us, but our God-ordained union equipped us to handle our personal and spiritual life.

Building a business from scratch demanded massive effort, but we persevered. We expanded to four studio rooms, twelve teachers, 147 weekly students, and an instrument showroom.

An angel partner agreed to join us in taking our seven-year-old business to the next level. We stood ready for this investment.

God had other plans—plans for prosperity and making Himself real to us.

God prepared us for ministry work—His ministry.

God calls, saves, and pursues you. His purpose always centers on rescue and salvation.

Would we heed this call, our own 'SOS'? The saving of our souls?

What you can do now: Celebrate your courage in taking new risks. Each small act of bravery—like making that phone call you fear—builds confidence. Consider writing down these courageous moments to remind yourself of your strength on difficult days.

Finding True Freedom from Control

Since my 'Independence Day'—Perseus' death—I began recognizing the church's control, occasionally questioning and rebelling. My rebellion didn't reject God's will but opposed leadership's control over every aspect of my natural and spiritual life and our home. Leadership still demanded obedience and micromanagement. My husband started noticing this too.

One example: early in our marriage, my husband took me to Hawaii for our anniversary, clearing this first with leadership. A month later, on my mother's birthday, my husband asked if I could travel out of state to celebrate with her. Leadership refused, saying we'd already missed enough church.

Another example: leadership micromanaged my church music involvement. While visiting another church during their convention, they invited me to sit on the platform with other pianists. My pastor objected, instructing me to lie that I needed to sit with my boys in the congregation. My husband and their grandmother were present, so I wasn't actually needed there. I believe the visiting pastor's wife understood what I couldn't say aloud. This broke my heart; I sat with my boys, crying bitter tears. My seat remained empty on the platform for the rest of that meeting. This event bonded my heart to the lovely woman who had invited me to join them.

At one point, we both quit. I stepped away from my music leadership, and Jonathan left his youth ministry and audio department roles. But cults don't allow legitimate reasons to leave—former followers are always characterized as wrong, negative, or even evil. This didn't last long; this was all we knew. Jonathan was a newborn when his parents moved their family to the Midwest for this church. We returned, repenting for leaving. Breaking free and feeling empowered to leave proves difficult when a cult maintains such control. Little did we know that our 'SOS' signal was already blinking in the atmosphere!

An autonomous affiliate church in the United Kingdom needed a Pastor. Jonathan and I separately heard God's call on our lives. When asked to take this position, we leapt at it. In the past, leadership had 'sent away' those who questioned authority.

Was this our case? Nevertheless, we prepared to follow the Lord's call.

What you can do now: Identify where control patterns from your past might still affect your decision-making today. List situations where you still seek unnecessary permission or approval. Practice making small decisions independently and notice how it feels to trust your own judgment.

Embracing New Beginnings Beyond Familiar Boundaries

I changed my business plan and informed my angel investor partner about our London move. As we prepared, we encountered obstacles that made us question God's will. This drove me to pray earnestly.

The day before closing on our business, a document appeared that would halt and alter the sale.

I fasted and continued praying. We prepared to leave everything familiar, wanting to ensure this was right. I spread all the business sale papers across our living room floor, fell on my face, and prayed.

I opened our family Bible to Deuteronomy 4:29: *"But from there you will seek the LORD your God and you will find Him, if you search after Him with all your heart and with all your soul."* (Deuteronomy 4:29)

In Matthew 7:7, Jesus offers hope: *"Ask, and it will be given to you; seek, and you will find; knock, and it will be opened to you."* (Matthew 7:7)

God spoke to me through His Word.

I waited...

The next day Jonathan met with the music store owners planning to buy our business. He explained everything; they consulted their lawyers.

Jonathan called me: "You can stop fasting." They signed the papers; the sale completed.

God heard and answered—a miracle! Next came our home, sold the first week we listed it for sale by owner, including most furniture.

London, here we come.

What you can do now: Consider your own healing journey. What would one small step forward look like for you? Perhaps it's reading the next chapter, reaching out to a friend, or simply acknowledging your pain. Whatever it is, know that you don't walk alone. Our healing workshops offer both the tools and the supportive community that make taking these brave next steps not just possible, but transformative.

Lessons Learned: Your Roadmap to Freedom

Through my journey from captivity to freedom, I've discovered that liberation rarely arrives as expected. For me, it came through a shocking death that initially felt like loss rather than freedom. Awakening to manipulation brought profound grief—anger, confusion, and sorrow for stolen years. These emotions aren't wrong; they prepare the ground where new life grows.

I teach in my workshops that healing happens in stages. My journal became my sanctuary until I was ready to close that chapter and step forward. Love after trauma feels disorienting at first. Jonathan's kindness contrasted sharply with the control I had mistaken for love.

Each step toward independence—from that first nervous phone call to opening my music store—required courage I didn't know I possessed. The first decisions without seeking permission felt terrifying, then exhilarating. My sons, business, and eventually our ministry became channels for restoration, proving that joy itself is an act of resistance against darkness.

Though my journey began with tears, it blossomed into a life more beautiful than I dared imagine—evidence that new beginnings await anyone brave enough to step through freedom's open door.

CHAPTER 7
London & Truth

"As each stone was laid in front of me, I carefully walked on this path. At times, it was slow and unsteady. Unbeknownst to me, it was my path of freedom, that was leading me to the truth." – Bridget

†

Hoping for a new life and to serve Jesus, we crossed the Atlantic to share our passion with a new congregation. We'd left everything behind with only a few possessions and our precious boys, 5 and 7 years old. For them, we wanted a better life. A life-changing encounter awaited us—we didn't know what it looked like, but we were willing to learn and trusted God had opened this door for a new beginning.

I developed a love-hate relationship with England. I loved the culture, but hated how far we were from family and familiar things. London felt noisy, dirty, crowded, and filled with so many accents that made my head spin—all within the English language! This differed dramatically from our suburban Midwest life with its orderly, clean, quiet neighborhoods. The pristine, level cement sidewalks of my Midwest home became a distant memory as I walked England's pavements, sometimes centuries-old cobblestones.

Narrow streets, roundabouts, and close row houses became our new normal. We jumped right in, doing our best to blend with the locals. This expensive place became our home. We settled in a flat (called an apartment in America), which resembled more of a townhouse. We learned to use various public transit options, walked everywhere, and learned to shop locally with a trolley (called a buggy in America) until Jonathan could get a car.

The path to freedom often requires physical distance from toxic environments before we can see clearly enough to speak our truth. As someone who now guides survivors through this journey, I can show you how new environments become catalysts for the breakthrough moments that change everything.

Building Meaningful Community Connections

Our new church consisted mostly of immigrants from Africa—Uganda, Zimbabwe, Kenya, Nigeria—and a few British locals. They lovingly welcomed us and introduced us to their diverse cultures. We enjoyed their tasty foods. Their contagious enthusiasm when singing and worshipping in church captivated me.

I felt at home with this small congregation, despite missing America. They became my people, my spiritual children. The church provided housing and a modest salary, insufficient for survival in this expensive town. Strict visa restrictions allowed only church-based support for Jonathan.

I needed employment. I searched for work, inquiring at Harrods' music department. Nigel probably thought I was a crazy American asking for a job, but he provided a contact that led to my position selling pianos at the local department store. This full-time job meant Jonathan would homeschool our boys while I worked—a new venture for him. He committed to making our UK move successful for both our family and the church.

Discovering Your Authentic Voice

I began finding my voice in England and experiencing greater freedom. I rebuilt my teaching studio and furthered my music education at the Royal Schools of Music.

This liberating period allowed me to experience England's educational process. I delighted in mingling with fellow students—making music, composing, and learning concepts to become the best music teacher possible. Jonathan ensured I seized these educational opportunities.

Unlike my past, Jonathan encouraged my growth and dreams instead of hindering them. God restored me, mending each broken piece one by one.

I've learned that reclaiming education and personal interests is often the first step toward finding your authentic voice after abuse.

What you can do now: Consider what interests or educational pursuits you might have set aside because of others' control or expectations. Choose one area to explore or develop, even in a small way. Education and personal growth are powerful tools for reclaiming your authentic self.

Embracing a People-Centered Faith Community

Pastoring in the UK provided our first mission experience. The dynamics and cultural clashes created a learning experience for Jonathan and me. We wanted to establish a healthy church with Jesus at its center. We thought we understood what this should look like, but whenever we tried implementing concepts from our American church, God placed obstacles before us.

One concept we desperately clung to was having our own worship and gathering place. This proved impossible because of zoning laws and noise restrictions—we were a lively group that loved worship with singing and instruments.

Properties and land for churches came at prohibitive prices. We resigned ourselves to renting a hall (what Americans would call a room). God taught us a powerful lesson: it wasn't about the building but about the people. This contradicted our previous experience.

In America, everything centered on land and property investments. The worship place became central, hosting all events. Small groups didn't exist—only the big group mattered. Multiple weekly meetings kept congregants at this location for every church service and function.

Many healthy churches have beautiful buildings while still encouraging small groups and Bible studies outside their church building. This wasn't the case in my former group— an unhealthy practice. Everything happened at headquarters, preventing cliques or special groups from forming.

The contrast became stark. In healthy spiritual communities, the focus stays on people rather than institutions or buildings. Leaders serve rather than demand service. Genuine relationships flourish outside of controlled settings, and people have freedom to question and grow. No one person controls all aspects of spiritual life, and individual needs and circumstances receive genuine care.

In unhealthy spiritual environments like the one I'd left behind, everything centered on one building or location. Leadership demanded constant attendance and availability. Outside relationships were discouraged as cliques or threats. Questioning was seen as disloyalty or weakness. One leader controlled all aspects of members' lives, and individual needs were subordinated to institutional demands.

Healthy spiritual communities enhance rather than restrict personal growth and relationships outside the institution. This was the kind of community we were learning to build in England.

God built His church His way, not according to human frameworks. We learned to walk in love and focus on those we ministered to. This wasn't a physical building made of bricks and mortar. Walking in love meant becoming Jesus' hands and feet.

Jesus' words to Peter, *"Do you love me?"* in John 21:17 (ESV) actually irritated Peter. Jesus asked this question three times, beginning with, *"Do you love me more than these?"*

Peter replied, *"Yes, you know that I love you."* Jesus' response revealed an unfolding lesson about demonstrating this love. He said, *"Feed my lambs."*

This shepherd metaphor conveyed the responsibility of caring for the sheepfold, beginning with the most vulnerable—lambs that would die without timely feeding because of limited energy reserves. The second response after asking Peter again if he loved Him was *"Tend my sheep."* After the third time, *"Feed my sheep."*

Loving God's lambs and sheep—His people, the vulnerable, hungry, and needy—means loving, tending to, and feeding His people. This is what it means to love Jesus above all else.

How could we keep our congregation close when they scattered across London and surrounding boroughs? We went to them—their communities and homes. We started mid-week house meetings where my heart grew to love these people. I felt privileged to enter their living rooms and sitting rooms. Bible studies, tea and biscuits, and a cappella singing characterized these intimate gatherings. I treasured taking part in their hospitality and getting to know everyone who opened their home. We experienced Jesus' words recorded in Matthew:

"For where two or three are gathered in my name, there am I among them." (Matthew 18:20 ESV)

God wanted to lead His body, His people, His sheep. We needed to step aside and walk with God as He guided us.

Jonathan, determined not to repeat the American leadership's mistakes, preached about honesty. This message transformed our small congregation. Many immigrants faced visa issues, and the time had come for honesty with God and accountability.

This message permeated individual lives, inspiring everyone to walk with God authentically. No more hiding—walking with true integrity and following our Heavenly Father in every aspect of life, seen and unseen.

Though autonomous, our little English church still faced control attempts from American leadership. God sent many to help us during our transition. We didn't realize how our church and mission work would eventually change.

We built strong friendships with visitors from American, German, Dutch, Polish, and British churches. These sweet fellowship moments helped us through periods of loneliness. Yes, we shed many tears adjusting to life in a foreign country, but joyous laughter provided great comfort.

What you can do now: Reflect on how past experiences have shaped your understanding of love and service. Write down three ways that genuine love differs from control disguised as care. Practice expressing care for others in ways that respect their autonomy and dignity.

Finding Freedom Through Painful Truth

When abuse allegations surfaced in an American church, it disrupted our affiliated group. Rumors about my former Midwest church prompted Jonathan's questions. He asked, "Have you ever had an abortion?"

Of course, I hadn't—my abuser had been sterilized, preventing pregnancy, but Jonathan didn't know this. I'd kept this secret for years. This is what abusers do—command you to keep the secret to your grave. But my abuser was losing his hold on my life. The time had come to share by telling my story.

I told him.

I told him everything. I felt compelled to hold nothing back. He directly asked about my secret past, and it was time he knew ALL of it. My painful past contained sexual abuse, lies, and coverups. It wasn't an affair—it was clergy abuse by his uncle.

No more coverups. Time for the truth.

It poured out like a flood, accompanied by overwhelming grief. I felt relieved to share this secret I'd locked away. I told him the truth. No more deceit, no more lies—my first brave step. He became the first person I told. I mourned losing my firsts that should have belonged to Jonathan. The missing pieces now fit together for him. I couldn't stop crying. Somehow, the tears cleansed me, washing away horrific memories through this tsunami of lament.

I found liberation in opening this long-slammed door.

Part of me died that day as a new me came to life.

The time had come for my release—to trust the man who truly loved me, my husband, Jonathan. The truth was spoken by me. No longer was I silenced. I'd thought I'd found my voice through my new life and freedom in marrying Jonathan and moving to the UK.

Those were just whispers.

This time, I truly found my voice.

In my workshops with survivors, I've learned that this moment—telling your truth to someone safe—is where real healing begins. The breakthrough happens when silence is finally broken in the context of genuine love.

As the weight of decades fell away in that moment of truth-telling, I began to understand what healing really required. The intensity of finally releasing those memories felt overwhelming, and I tried to capture those feelings in the next poem.

Releasing Memories

It is confounding and disturbing how memories can
be tucked away.
Like Pandora's box, once opened, things locked away
jump out, creating a surge of release, feeling like a
pandemic to your soul, sickening you with its toxins
like contagions overtaking the good memories.
This is the danger of locking away, pushing aside, not
accepting, denying, things that have been done to
you, things that have violated you.
I'm finding my healing in the release of these
memories, opening up that box that has been sealed,
releasing the toxins, becoming inoculated from this
emotional pandemic of abuse.
Each unlocked and voiced memory leaves behind an
immunity to this debilitating disease with its toxins.
I have a choice, and I choose to no longer live with this.
I will rise up, unlock these memories, share so others
may step forward and embrace their healing.
As with any pandemic, it takes time for it to wane
and recover.
I must take it, one step at a time, unleashing the
memories, like antibodies, seeking the redemption
of my damaged spirit.

—Bridget Goodwin, 2021

Lessons Learned: The Breakthrough Moment

Looking back now, I can see how every piece of this journey worked together to bring me to that moment of truth-telling with Jonathan.

Physical distance from toxic environments created the perspective I needed to see clearly. My move to England provided new surroundings where I could grow authentically. The cultural contrasts highlighted what hadn't been normal in my previous setting. This separation preceded my courage to question deeply ingrained beliefs and finally tell my truth. Building a new life physically removed from the place of trauma gave me the space I needed to heal.

I discovered that healthy ministry differs fundamentally from what I'd experienced. True spiritual leadership empowers rather than controls. Authentic community centers on people, not buildings or institutions. Genuine spiritual growth thrives without micromanagement, and service flows from love rather than obligation or fear. In this healthier environment, my personal growth flourished—my education, new skills, and expanded horizons would have threatened the controlling structures of my past. Pursuing education and interests previously denied became part of my recovery.

The supportive relationship with Jonathan encouraged my development, helping me find my voice first in one area, then in speaking the truth about my past. My growth would have posed a threat to those invested in my limitation. Finding supportive, loving relationships that encourage growth, having space to develop authentic personal identity, and experiencing freedom to make independent choices—these became the foundation of my healing.

Through Jonathan's loving response to my painful revelation, I learned that truth emerges in safe relationships. His genuine love created safety for my honesty. The secret lost its power when shared with someone trustworthy. His unconditional acceptance allowed buried truths to surface after decades of silence.

Breaking free completely required finding the courage to tell my whole truth, allowing myself to grieve losses fully, and accepting that healing involves painful revelations. What initially felt like weakness—my vulnerability in sharing my story—became strength in the context of love. Recognizing that genuine love creates safety for honesty changed everything. I learned that my voice gets stronger with each telling. Taking the risk to be fully known led to deeper liberation, clearing the way for authentic connection in our marriage and setting the stage for healing that would continue to unfold in the years ahead.

What you can do now: If you're carrying secrets from past trauma, consider who might be a safe person to share your story with. Remember that healing often occurs in trustworthy relationships. The act of speaking your truth—even to one person—can begin breaking the power of silence. Professional counseling can provide a protected space for this process.

If you're ready to find your voice and tell your truth, you're not alone in this journey. Connect with other survivors who understand this breakthrough moment at ihaveavoice.love, where we create safe spaces specifically designed for truth-telling and healing. Your voice matters, and your healing is possible.

I was able to identify my trauma, naming each bar of my cage. I'll share how this breakthrough moment of truth-telling opened the floodgates for deeper healing and how finding my voice in one area empowered me to speak up in others. The journey from breaking silence to reclaiming power was just beginning, but this moment with Jonathan became the foundation for everything that followed.

CHAPTER 8
London Bridge is Falling Down

"My voice has broken the sound barrier of my assailant. It has boomed, breaking the waves of shame and deceit. My world has been rocked, but I step in the light of my deliverance." – Bridget

†

The truth was out, and it had rocked our world and our marriage. I had massive amounts of baggage that needed to be unpacked, discarded, and demolished. My loving husband stood by my side and gave me his unconditional love. What an example of true love he displayed to me. Jonathan held me, dried my tears, and reassured me of his undying love.

Our marriage had taken a blow, yet Jonathan relentlessly worked through the many questions he asked me. It was shocking and disturbing, but I was solaced by his comfort. This was liberation for me—but for my husband, it was a huge revealing of his life, his wife, and our involvement with the church group in the Midwest where we had come from. I was very aware this wasn't easy for my husband.

I was no longer held captive by Perseus. I broke the agreement that I was to die with this horrendous secret of his sexual involvement and deceptions.

Understanding why victims stay silent took me decades to grasp. Research consistently shows that clergy sexual abuse affects approximately 3.0% of women churchgoers (Chaves & Garland, 2009). Research shows that disclosure of sexual abuse is rarely immediate—almost half of survivors wait over five years before telling anyone, and some never do (Elliot, et al).

Clergy who commit sexual misconduct often use calculated grooming tactics rather than overt physical force. They may offer special attention, invoke spiritual or religious justification, and gradually blur emotional and physical boundaries to normalize increasingly inappropriate behavior. Because of their spiritual authority and trusted position, clergy can exert powerful psychological and emotional influence that leaves victims feeling spiritually conflicted, dependent, and unable to refuse or report the abuse. Baylor University's research emphasizes that these dynamics constitutes an abuse of power and trust—not a consensual relationship—and must be recognized as clergy sexual misconduct. (Baylor University School of Social Work, 2018)

Many victims don't speak up because they don't realize what they're experiencing is actually abuse. They're made to feel the relationship is consensual, which it isn't. Perpetrators threaten victims into silence by claiming they'll commit suicide if the victim leaves, or that the ministry will be devastated and ruined. Leaders twist religious texts to convince victims that the sexual behavior is allowed by God.

The reality of victim blaming and shaming is another major deterrent. Many choose to avoid being retraumatized by keeping the abuse secret, even after it has ended. When victims witness others being blamed, shamed, and disbelieved, it sends a clear message that speaking up is dangerous.

Decades later I was brave enough to speak. Jonathan's compassion and unwillingness to judge me gave me that safe haven that started my healing journey. As I began telling my story to my husband, my grief turned to anger. I realized this was sexual abuse and manipulation. The brainwashing vanished as each angry, anguished tear was shed in my sobbing.

My emotions and logic were twisted by my abuser.

I was not an adult—I was 13 years old.

I was targeted, called "special."

I was vulnerable, called "trustworthy."

This was not love, this was rape!

I was finally being set free from this bad person, and I was furious that he took advantage of me.

His control was being broken.

It was time to tell and this poem captures the significance of your voice being set free.

Tell and Warn

Why tell?
Why let the secret out?
To break the chain and unlock the victim.
Breaking the silence, shedding the light of the truth
into the deep cavern of darkness filled with deceits,
this is why!
Stop the cycle, the threat, let your voice be heard,
"No more!"
The abuser doesn't love you, actually he hates you,
because he is destroying you."
Be brave, you are safe now!"
Replace every lie with truth, every link in the chain
that weighs heavy on you is being broken.
Step into the glorious light, run from the darkness,
your chains are gone!
Now warn, help others out of this darkness!

—Bridget Goodwin, 2021

Closer Than Ever

What could have driven us apart instead brought Jonathan and me closer than ever. The third party—Perseus lurking behind that shut door—was now gone. So many things started to make sense to Jonathan. This was the beginning of Perseus falling from the pedestal that Jonathan had put him on. What Jonathan didn't know was that the church system was falling apart as well.

My husband needed solace because his world was falling apart, so he spoke to the current leader in the Midwest church. This was spoken to him: "You have to separate the man from the message." Jonathan knew immediately not to accept this.

This attempt to separate the sinful man from his teaching is a common deflection tactic in abusive religious systems. It suggests that somehow the "truth" a person speaks can remain pure while their character is corrupt. But a poisoned well cannot produce clean water. The messages Perseus preached were shaped by the same distorted thinking that allowed him to abuse children and manipulate an entire congregation. His theology served his pathology.

When an abusive leader delivers messages about submission, authority, and God's judgment, these teachings are inherently tainted by their need to control others. Perseus didn't just happen to be a predator who also taught sound doctrine—his doctrine was crafted specifically to enable his predatory behavior and shield him from accountability.

Jonathan understood this instinctively. How could we trust any teaching from a man who had so completely betrayed the most fundamental truths of the faith? How could we believe the words of someone who used those very words to manipulate, control, and abuse?

He knew this was unbiblical, just as in the story of Achan in Joshua 7:1. Achan did not regard the devoted things taken from Jericho and hid them with his possessions. This was against the command of God—these possessions belonged to God. Right before the walls of Jericho fell, God told Israel in Joshua 6:18-19, *"but you, keep yourselves from the things devoted to destruction, lest when you have devoted them you take any of the devoted things and make the camp of Israel a thing for destruction and bring trouble upon it. But all silver and gold, and every vessel of bronze and iron, are holy unto the LORD; they shall go to the treasury for the LORD."*

God was fully aware of what was happening in the camp of Israel. You may think that you can hide, but you cannot—God sees it and that which is done in secret will be revealed. God stands by His Word:

"For God will bring every deed into judgment, with every secret thing, whether good or evil." (Ecclesiastes 12:14 ESV)

God will not tolerate that Israel had sinned and lied, and God was not pleased. Joshua 7 reads:

The Lord said to Joshua, "Get up! Why have you fallen on your face? Israel has sinned; they have transgressed my covenant that I commanded them; they have taken some of the devoted things; they have stolen and lied and put them among their own belongings. Therefore the people of Israel cannot stand before their enemies. They turn their backs before their enemies, because they have become devoted for destruction. I will be with you no more, unless you destroy the devoted things from among you. Get up! Consecrate the people and say, 'Consecrate yourselves for tomorrow; for thus says the Lord, God of Israel, "There are devoted things in your midst, O Israel. You cannot stand before your enemies until you take away the devoted things from among you." (Joshua 7:10-13 ESV)

God's mandate required the actions of the people to be righteous—you can't do the right thing the wrong way. No one is exempt, neither the leader nor the people.

The System That Protects Abusers

Jonathan could see that the ethos of the church group was more about protecting the leadership of the past than the congregants who were still part of the group. It had been over 10 years since Perseus' death. These lies had crept into the church and became the foundation on which it still stood. If the leader is corrupt, then how could the message be pure? The real enemy was the sin.

Research shows a disturbing pattern in how religious institutions respond when abuse comes to light. According to the 2017 Royal Commission into Institutional Responses to Child Sexual Abuse, leaders of religious institutions frequently responded to victims' reports of abuse with disbelief, denial, or attempts to blame or discredit the victim, often prioritizing the protection of the institution's reputation over justice or care for survivors. Researchers have documented a pattern of institutional protection within religious organizations—transferring accused clergy instead of removing them, concealing allegations from congregations and civil authorities, and pressuring victims to forgive without accountability, (Royal Commission into Institutional Responses to Child Sexual Abuse 2017).

The system was designed to protect itself at all costs. When allegations of abuse emerge, there's a predictable pattern.

First comes denial: *"That couldn't have happened here."*

Then comes minimization: *"Maybe something happened, but it wasn't as bad as they're saying."*

Next comes victim-blaming: *"They must have misunderstood or contributed to the situation."*

Finally comes institutional preservation: *"We need to handle this quietly to protect the ministry."*

This is exactly what happened with our church. The current leaders knew there had been problems, but addressing them fully would require dismantling the entire foundation their authority rested on. They would have to admit that the special group, the bride members concept was built on a corrupt foundation. They would have to acknowledge that they had been part of a system that enabled abuse rather than protected the vulnerable.

The financial implications were enormous. If people recognized the depth of corruption, they would leave. Tithes would drop. The expensive building that symbolized their specialness might be lost. The comfortable positions of authority would dissolve.

So instead, they chose to compartmentalize: "Separate the man from the message." This convenient fiction allowed them to preserve the system while appearing to acknowledge wrongdoing. But you cannot separate a person's character from their teaching when that teaching was specifically crafted to enable their misconduct.

Ronald Enroth writes in Churches That Abuse about five categories of abuse. One describes how authority gets twisted: "Abuse arises when leaders of a group arrogate to themselves power and authority that lacks the dynamics of open accountability and the capacity to question or challenge decisions made by leaders. The shift entails moving from general respect for an office bearer to one where members loyally submit without any right to dissent."

God's principles are not about protecting sin with lies, but about exposing it and repenting of it.

Jonathan's nagging doubts became realities—Perseus was not the man he thought he was. He was actually very evil. Fear of exposing the immorality and wickedness of the past leadership causes the current leadership to bury their heads in the sand. Once the congregants realize the depth of depravity, they will begin to see that they aren't the special group, the bride members that they thought they were. At this point the fear of members leaving and joining other churches is too great. Who will then give tithes and offerings to keep the brick-and-mortar building going, and pay the salaries of the staff?

The fear really comes down to the money, and losing the building and property—and then it's the loss of position and power.

Jonathan and I could see that this had impacted everything in our spiritual lives.

God was rebuilding our belief system. What was not of Him was being demolished.

The Body Keeps the Score

My secret was out to only Jonathan, and the emotional trauma that kept score in my body was showing up in my stomach. According to Psychologist Stephen W. Porges, trauma can become embedded in the autonomic nervous system such that the body continues to hold the experience even when conscious awareness is limited. Put simply, trauma stays in the body even if one is not aware of it.

Dr. Bessel van der Kolk's book, *The Body Keeps the Score*, research shows that trauma gets stored physically in the body, not just in the mind. The landmark ACE Study (Adverse Childhood Experiences Study) conducted by Kaiser Permanente and the CDC found that childhood trauma connects strongly with adult health problems. (Felitti et al., 1998). Sexual trauma specifically has been linked to gastrointestinal disorders. Up to 44% of patients with IBS or functional gastrointestinal disorders report histories of sexual trauma (Drossman, 2011).

Peter Levine explains in *Waking the Tiger* that when we bury trauma instead of processing it, the body doesn't forget. It can show up as physical tension, pain, or symptoms that medicine alone can't explain. This explains why trauma survivors may experience physical improvement when they begin addressing their psychological trauma.

While I had mentally compartmentalized my abuse for decades, my body never forgot. My stomach issues weren't coincidental or just a reaction to British food—they were my body's physical record of trauma. The chronic stomach pain, digestive issues, and unexplained symptoms were my body's way of saying "something is wrong" when my conscious mind couldn't face the truth. Every unexplained pain, every visit to the doctor that yielded no clear diagnosis—these were echoes of trauma seeking acknowledgment.

I may have unlocked my sexual trauma, but what about the physical score of trauma locked away? I needed healing emotionally but also physically. I didn't grasp the damage that my body had taken. My body was crying out for help. I thought I had developed an intolerance to British food. Maybe it was IBS, or gluten, or at one point I thought I had a bleeding ulcer. After several GP (General Practitioner as they are called in the UK) visits to find out, antacids were prescribed and I kept strong peppermints at hand.

I believed I could manage the physical symptoms on my own—a common misconception I now recognize in many survivors. What I didn't understand was that acknowledging my trauma would be my first step to genuine healing.

The weight of it all—the physical symptoms, the emotional processing, the uncertainty about what came next—pressed down on me constantly. I captured those overwhelming feelings in a poem during one of my darkest moments.

Fight or Flight

Yesterday I physically felt sick, like I was going to toss my cookies.
Was it the therapy session?
Was it the summary of my husband's session?
Was it because my dad had to go to the hospital?
I'm starting to be acutely aware of how the body reacts physically to emotional stress.
Am I going to fight, or flight?
I wonder if I'm going to make it, can I rise above this?\I feel numb.
Will I survive this pandemic of my spirit?

—Bridget Goodwin, 2021

Mission Fields

During all of this we were still pastoring our little flock in the UK. I worked closely with my husband in our ministry. My heart was being nurtured as I helped others in their struggles. I cried, rejoiced and celebrated every moment of their lives. I learned to pray, taking time when I hit the running trails to mention each name and their needs to Jesus. Helping others helped me to heal.

We started visiting different countries spreading the gospel of Jesus. One testimony of answered prayer for China happened like this. I remember a burden for China came over me, and I felt that God was going to lead us there somehow. I started praying about it, reaching out to my friends, networking to see if we should connect with someone over there.

One night an intense feeling of prayer came over me, and I just prayed and wept. It was as if I could hear a group or someone praying for help in China. Later on I found out that a group was actually praying during a meeting at this time I felt this burden! I started to fast, asking God to show us if we should visit. I made a connection through one of my friends' networks.

I had my friends praying with me, I shared this burden with them. I remember I was discouraged that I wasn't receiving an answer to my prayer and fasting. Jonathan told me maybe I needed to change the way I was praying. If God gave me this burden, then I should pray that it would happen. That night something happened!

I received communication from a contact from one of my friends that had been praying with me. This lovely communication came with the question, "So tell me how the Holy Spirit is leading you?" WOW! She shared with me and told me she may have contacts for me. Within several days I received an email and it was in Chinese. At the end of the email, it was translated into English. We had made contact, and God opened the door and we visited Hong Kong, and Jonathan went into China.

As we traveled to Europe, Asia, and Africa, we really felt the call to the mission fields. We traveled with our boys and with friends. It was exciting sharing the name of Jesus and His power in our missionary work. It was a spiritual healing time for me, watching God work in the lives of those we encountered around the world. We stayed in their homes from India, Hong Kong, to Germany, Moldova and Poland.

We laughed and prayed together around their dinner table enjoying the delicious ethnic food steeped in the culture of their homeland. We worshiped God and shared the Word of God in their living rooms and church buildings. We worked with translators and musicians singing in English and their native tongue. The Spirit of God has no boundaries, there's room at the cross for all. I loved this new facet of our ministry, working in the fields and being with all nationalities. We founded our ministry called, Harvest Labourers International.

Jonathan had a love and care for the people that was in our pastoral care, and we began to see that it wasn't right to be traveling to the mission fields and pastoring at the same time. We couldn't be the pastors anymore looking at the long-term goal. We had one final step to our Visa. We had already spent thousands of pounds for our leave to remain status, but we were willing to let it go to follow God. We had given our time, heart and lives to these dear people, our congregation in England. One last step and that was to have dual citizenship.

We met some amazing supportive friends in the UK who counseled us and prayed with us regarding our thoughts about our future ministry. God was talking to us through others as well that we needed to make a change. We were suffering, our marriage was trying to cope with my sexual trauma, and Jonathan needed help to carry me. Our eyes were further opened when we could see how the group was holding us captive spiritually. We needed to break free from them, and their control. Even though we were autonomous, the current leader of this Midwest Group would call Jonathan and tell him how to handle me when we went to church events in the US.

The instructions were deeply troubling and revealed how the control continued even across an ocean. The leader would tell Jonathan things like:

"If asked to play the piano at church conventions, tell her to decline"—controlling who I could interact with.

"Don't let her be the band director/play the piano when you're visiting a certain church"—controlling my ministry of music.

"If you fellowship those people (those that had been disfellowshipped from the group) we will visit you less in England"—isolating us from those who might validate our concerns.

"If you let people (those that had been disfellowshipped from the group) sit on the platform during your convention, some ministers will get up and leave during your service"—controlling us with threats, monitoring our relationships.

These pastoral instructions weren't about my spiritual wellbeing—they were about maintaining control over me and Jonathan's ministry.

This disfellowship from the group was not because of sin, but because the leadership of this precious group of people was listening to the direction of God, and wouldn't put on his people the burden and yoke of man's ideology. One example, women wearing trousers, to some this is a sin, but in fact this is a tradition of man set on the people. God was starting to liberate His people in this church, and the leadership was seeking God, and they were disfellowshipped! God was moving in a great way, and it has been evident through the years that what God has called clean is not unclean.

I have said it before, where the Spirit of the Lord is, there is freedom.

Our Marriage After the Truth

When I revealed my abuse to Jonathan, we entered uncharted territory in our relationship. What could have destroyed us instead created a deeper bond, but the journey wasn't simple or straightforward.

Jonathan experienced a whirlwind of emotions—shock at what had happened, anger toward Perseus and the system that enabled him, grief for what I had endured, and confusion about how this would affect our relationship. He questioned everything: "How could I not have known? What does this mean for us? How do I help her heal?"

For me, telling Jonathan felt like both a death and a rebirth. A part of me died that day—the part that had carried this secret alone for so many years—while something new was born: a relationship built on complete truth rather than partial disclosure.

We had to navigate new emotional terrain together. There were days when I couldn't stop crying, when the memories would flood back without warning. There were nights when sleep would be troubled with nightmares and I would wake up screaming. These times were difficult as we processed this new reality. There were painful conversations as Jonathan tried to understand the full extent of what had happened, and I struggled to articulate experiences I had buried for decades.

Yet through it all, we grew closer. The secret third party in our marriage—Perseus and his continued control over my past—was gone. For the first time, we were truly alone together, with nothing hidden between us. Jonathan's response—his unwavering support, his refusal to blame me, his commitment to stand with me—showed me what genuine love looked like.

Our marriage became stronger because it was now rooted in complete truth and authentic acceptance. This isn't to romanticize trauma or suggest that revealing abuse automatically improves relationships—many relationships don't survive such revelations. But for us, the truth, however painful, created the foundation for a deeper connection than we had ever known before.

Remember, "An untold story never heals." — Mary DeMuth

Finding Freedom

Our supportive friends and ministers in the UK, who were outside of our Midwest Group, wisely counseled us that if we didn't leave, we would lose our marriage and our health. Because we lived in another country, we were isolated, but it was to our advantage.

Living abroad allowed us to develop relationships with others in ministerial works. In these friendships, we found comfort and counsel. As we shared our lives and my past trauma, we learned more about the love of God. Shattered and broken, we knew we needed help.

It was so refreshing to unload our hearts to them as they lovingly showed us the way forward. They prayed with us to be delivered. Slowly, we could start to see that we had been part of a controlling group of people. Our answer was in breaking free from the Midwest Group. But how? I was scared—this was all we ever knew. Jonathan and I faced this together. He stood next to me as I coped with my sexual trauma. I would stand next to him as he looked for direction concerning his ministry and his family. Jonathan needed help to heal from church hurt and trauma.

Jonathan began his journey of healing from church hurt and made a bold step of his own—he stopped listening to the Midwest group and their demands, and started to listen to God on his own. Jonathan learned that living in England had been good for his Christian maturity because it had kept him from the group, even though it had been so very lonely. It was there in the UK for the past several years that he discovered who God was.

God was his Heavenly Father and God wasn't out to judge his every action in doom. God was there to care for His children, no malice was intended, no evil.

The scriptures lovingly state in the Words of Jesus, *"Which one of you, if his son asks him for bread, will give him a stone? Or if he asks for a fish, will give him a serpent? If you then, who are evil, know how to give good gifts to your children, how much more will your Father who is in heaven give good things to those who ask him!"* (Matthew 7:9-11 ESV)

Jonathan learned to be authentic to God. One day he was praying, telling God how he really felt and God responded, "Finally an honest prayer." We were the children of God, and this relationship with our Heavenly Father was developing.

From Fear-Based Religion to Truth-Based Faith

We grew up with a God who was watching us, and if something bad happened we would quote these phrases that were blasted from the pulpit:

"Shall not the judge of all earth do what is just?"—This phrase from Genesis 18:25 was twisted from Abraham's plea for mercy into a warning that God would punish any perceived wrongdoing. Instead of emphasizing God's justice being tempered with mercy, it became a threat that divine punishment was always imminent for the slightest misstep.

"Is there not a cause?"—Taken from David's response in 1 Samuel 17:29, this phrase was weaponized to shame anyone who questioned leadership decisions. Any hesitation or doubt was portrayed as a lack of faith or commitment to the cause, effectively silencing legitimate concerns.

"Judgment must first begin at the house of God."—This partial quote from 1 Peter 4:17 was frequently used to justify harsh treatment of congregation members. Rather than encouraging self-examination, it became a tool for leaders to criticize, control, and manipulate through fear of divine punishment.

"After the first or second admonition reject."—This fragment from Titus 3:10 was applied broadly to anyone who raised questions or concerns. The original context about divisive people was expanded to include anyone who didn't fully comply with leadership dictates, creating a culture where questioning meant risking complete rejection and isolation.

These phrases weren't merely quoted—they were wielded as weapons. These quotes from God's Holy Word were twisted and created an atmosphere of constant anxiety, where God was portrayed as primarily angry, always watching for mistakes, and eager to punish. Every difficulty was interpreted as divine judgment, every illness as potential punishment, every question as dangerous rebellion.

Such fear and terror were in our hearts. These voices became a continual struggle, but we learned to put these lies on trial and replace them with God's truths.

"Surely goodness and mercy shall follow me all the days of my life." (Psalms 23:6 ESV)

"I believe that I shall look upon the goodness of the Lord in the land of the living!" (Psalms 27:13 ESV)

"Oh, taste and see that the Lord is good! Blessed is the man who takes refuge in him!" (Psalms 34:8 ESV)

The process of replacing fear with truth wasn't instantaneous. It involved reconsidering everything we had been taught about God's nature. We had to intentionally challenge each fearful thought with scriptures that revealed God's true character—not as a threatening tyrant, but as a loving Father. Each verse about God's goodness, patience, and kindness became a stepping stone away from fear and toward authentic faith.

We were moving forward and had no idea. God again was opening doors for our freedom.

Recognizing the Warning Signs

Spiritual Manipulation:
- Scripture used to block professional help
- Suffering framed as God keeping you humble
- Mental health treated as spiritual failure
- Medication or therapy shamed

Re-Victimization:
- "Are you sure?"
- "Why didn't you speak up sooner?"
- "They're dead, so what now?"
- "If" statements casting doubt
- Protecting reputation over victims

Institutional Resistance:
- Refusing independent investigations
- Vague statements minimizing abuse
- Profiting from abusers' materials
- Silencing victims through intimidation
- Framing abuse as isolated, not systemic

Boundary Violations:
- Controlling decisions despite distance
- Spiritual threats ("lose your salvation")
- Blocking independent relationships and support

Lessons Learned

Looking back on this season of our lives, I can see now what I couldn't see then—that every painful revelation, every moment of doubt, every step toward freedom was leading us somewhere better. The journey from silence to speaking, from captivity to liberation, from fear to faith taught me truths I want to share with you.

Truth liberates, even when painful. Revealing long-held secrets can be terrifying, but it's often the first essential step toward healing. When I finally told Jonathan my secret, the weight I'd carried alone for decades became lighter because I was no longer carrying it by myself.

The act of speaking my truth out loud helped me recognize the manipulation for what it was. For years, I'd believed Perseus's lies about our "relationship." But when I heard myself say the words "I was thirteen" to my husband, something shifted. Facing reality, however painful, gave me the power to change it.

Authentic relationships survive truth. I was so afraid that telling Jonathan would destroy our marriage. Instead, it saved it. Genuine love can withstand even the most difficult revelations. Our relationship became stronger because it was now built on honesty and transparency rather than secrecy.

True intimacy only became possible when my whole self was known and accepted. God brought Jonathan into my life—someone who could handle my truth without judgment, someone who would stand beside me rather than run away.

Healing is holistic—mind, body, and spirit. I learned this the hard way. Trauma affected me physically, not just emotionally and mentally. My body kept the score even when my mind tried to forget. Those years of stomach issues, the unexplained pain, the symptoms that wouldn't respond to treatment—my body was signaling a truth my mind had buried. Physical healing began when I finally acknowledged my emotional wounds. Complete healing required addressing all dimensions of trauma, not just the parts I was ready to face.

God's character versus manipulated religion became crystal clear to me during this time. The abusive religious system had twisted scripture to create fear, but healing required finding God's true character. Where religious trauma had created fear in my heart, God's love became the antidote. I discovered that healthy faith empowers rather than controls. The journey from fear-based to love-based faith was challenging but liberating. Every fearful phrase I'd heard from the pulpit had to be replaced with the truth of who God really is—not an angry judge waiting to punish, but a loving Father ready to heal.

Freedom came in stages, not all at once. Breaking free from the controlling system happened in steps. Physical distance—our move to England—created space for perspective I couldn't have gained while still immersed in the group. Living in another country allowed us to see patterns of control we'd accepted as normal. Recognizing these patterns was the first step to breaking them.

Each small act of independence built confidence for greater freedom. Jonathan's decision to stop listening to the Midwest group's demands and start listening to God on his own was one of those brave steps. My decision to share my story publicly was another.

Community healing brings restoration. Years later, when I began hosting workshops through, I Have a Voice ministries, I witnessed something profound: collective healing happens when survivors share their stories together. There's something sacred about sitting in a circle with other women who understand the weight of secrets, the courage required to speak, and the long journey toward freedom.

Each testimony shared becomes medicine for someone else's wound. When one woman finds her voice, it gives permission for another to find hers. I've seen decades of shame dissolve in a single afternoon when survivors realize they're not alone, not crazy, and not damaged beyond repair. This communal aspect of healing—bearing witness to each other's truth—creates ripples of restoration that extend far beyond our individual journeys.

If you're reading this and recognizing your own story in mine, know this: freedom is possible. The chains that have held you can be broken. The silence that has protected your abuser can be shattered. The lies you've believed about yourself can be replaced with truth. It won't happen overnight, and it won't be easy, but it will be worth it.

God was opening doors for our freedom, and we were finally ready to walk through them.

What you can do now: Identify a religious phrase or belief from your past that created fear rather than hope. Write it down, then research its biblical context to understand how it may have been twisted. Next to it, write a scripture that reveals God's true loving character. When that fearful thought returns, speak the truth-based scripture aloud. This practice helps rewire your understanding of God's nature from fear-based to love-based, supporting your spiritual healing journey.

CHAPTER 9
Hard Healing

"I no longer have the strength to fight. I must fly away where I can find peace." – Bridget

†

Triggers surrounded me during my life in England. As a pastor's wife, women's leader, and worship director, I struggled to cope with my sexual trauma. Movies reduced me to sobs as I relived my past experiences. My mind had unlocked buried memories, and they flooded me until I felt I was drowning in tears. Sights, sounds, and smells pushed me into flight mode. For years, I'd fought to keep these memories locked away. Now, the triggers intensified, creating increasing struggles for both me and Jonathan.

The healing process requires time—something I didn't fully understand then. My decades of abuse demanded a lengthy recovery journey. I had no idea what this would look like or how to begin.

The research below describes exactly what I experienced—walking in darkness but beginning to glimpse the light.

The Healing Journey of Sexual Trauma Survivors

Research by Judith Herman consistently shows that healing from sexual trauma isn't linear but occurs in stages. Survivors typically move through three phases: establishing safety, remembering and mourning, and reconnection with ordinary life.

Most survivors experience periods of progress followed by temporary setbacks.

Studies indicate that survivors who disclose their trauma in a supportive environment show better long-term outcomes than those who maintain secrecy. However, healing timelines vary dramatically. Recovery is influenced by pre-trauma psychological health, severity and duration of trauma, post-trauma support, and access to appropriate treatment.

The experience of being "triggered" is neurobiologically based. When trauma memories are activated, the brain's alarm system responds as if the danger is present again, triggering the fight, flight, or freeze response even in safe environments. (Van der Kolk, 2014).

What you can do now: Create a "trigger journal" to record when and how trauma memories surface. Note what preceded the trigger, your physical and emotional responses, and coping strategies that helped. This practice empowers you by converting unconscious reactions into conscious understanding, giving you more control over your healing journey.

During the painful period of recognizing triggers, I wrote this poem wrestling with how to process both painful and precious memories from my past.

Memories

How do you cope and separate the good from the bad?
Are there really any "good" memories?
These memories are tainted, poisoned, and horrific.
I feel like I'm looking through a microscope,
questioning every motive and action.
How do I deal with this?
Let the bad memories escape into the abyss.
Recall the good, build new memories, it is a choice.
Bitterness must not be my fuel.
Revenge must not be my drive.
Speak the truth and let mercy prevail.
Good memories will prevail.

—Bridget Goodwin, 2021

Making Life-Changing Decisions with Courage

As Jonathan and I navigated my triggers, we traveled to America. These triggers remained uncontrolled. A movie depicting a woman being assaulted or an older man taking advantage of a younger girl would put me on high alert. I carefully monitored what I watched or listened to. Any abuse storylines or character disturbances made me spiral.

Our good friends always hosted us in their home, and when they visited the UK, we reciprocated. We worked effectively together in ministry, and they provided tremendous encouragement during our missionary phase. Visiting America always offered rest and renewal. During this particular visit, God clearly revealed it was time to relocate. Our oldest son would attend university in the Carolinas, and we would move there to establish our new missionary ministry.

We returned to the UK and our London pastorate to prepare for our next life chapter. We explained our plans to our church and established procedures for them to continue without us. The new pastor and his wife already knew the congregation well and demonstrated genuine love for the people. The timing seemed right.

Though gut-wrenching for many—and not everyone understood—we needed to follow God's voice. Jonathan followed divine guidance, and we made this journey together. Just as God had opened the door for our UK mission, the time had come to walk through another door—our exit.

As we prepared for this major transition, doubt tried to trap me. I captured those feelings in this poem about breaking free from paralyzing uncertainty as I tried to heal.

My Doubts

My doubts today are like a web, sticky, and clinging to me.
It's evident this web of deceit has held me captive,
invading my mind.
It's time to be set free from this trap, it's many
threads of bondage.
It is okay to break the threads, to demolish this web.
Just as the sunbeams hi-light the intricate details of a
web, it takes the light of Jesus to see that these doubts
need to be taken down.
After all, it is just a fine thread of stickiness, yes, its
purpose is to catch its prey to devour as you become
immobile.
The spider waits until the struggle is over.
Just as the spider, the enemy waits as we struggle in
these fine strings of stickiness, wrapping us up.
Doubts, fears and what ifs suffocate us.
The light of Jesus shines and we can see an escape, it
is only an illusion, this death trap.
We can be set free; we must break loose as we can see
through the illuminating power of Christ's redemption.
Through Him we break through, shake off those
clinging doubts, guilt and fears.
He cleanses us lovingly with His healing waters of
forgiveness and hope.
He anoints our head with oil, our doubts are
released, we are filled with anticipation and joy.
We have seen the light!

—Bridget Goodwin, 2021

Facing Crisis While Healing

Stress overwhelmed Jonathan. The ministry demands, my trauma processing, our financial pressures—everything culminated in crisis. My young husband of 43 suffered a massive heart attack. We'd planned to leave for America in just two and a half months. How could this happen? I rode in the ambulance in a daze.

When the medic checked his vitals and ran the EKG, his dreaded words froze me: "He's having a heart attack."

My world stopped.

Questions and fears whirled through my mind. I couldn't imagine life without him. Would he die? How could this happen? He'd been losing weight and walking several miles daily. We'd both embarked on healing journeys, navigating life together. We could face this challenge—I just couldn't bear facing it alone. I needed him, and he needed me.

The medics explained they were taking him to Harefield Hospital, a premier heart center less than five miles away. We'd only recently moved to this Watford house, with no idea how providential this location would prove. Harefield Hospital ranks among the United Kingdom's top two cardiac facilities. God remained fully aware of our situation, arranging everything for Jonathan's care.

Hospital regulations prevented me from staying in the ward. Early morning, the nurses informed me I needed to leave before the 7:00 AM shift change. Unlike American private rooms, this public healthcare facility featured an open ward with separate rooms. The care proved exceptional! I remain forever grateful to Harefield Hospital's dedicated team.

I called a cab to take me home. Watching the same trees and roads the ambulance had traveled with my Johnny, I felt overwhelmed with gratitude. My prayers—and the many prayers from others that covered me like a comforting, loving blanket—had been answered. He survived!

Our boys, now old enough to stay home, received visits from church members who checked on them. When I arrived home, they were watching "The Simpsons"—a welcome distraction for them. I collapsed into bed, clinging to my refuge chapter, Psalms 91, especially verse 2: *"I will say to the LORD, 'My refuge and my fortress, my God, in whom I trust."* (ESV).

I needed others' prayers; though I prayed, I felt numb. I clung to God, hoping and finding shelter in Him. Two dear American friends stayed on the phone with me throughout my waiting room vigil. Hearing their voices provided tremendous comfort in my isolation. I knelt to pray, and a compassionate medic entered to reassure me they were taking excellent care of Jonathan. His hopeful demeanor comforted me.

Since it was Wednesday evening after our Merstham Bible study, precious church members rushed to support me. Hours later, when the doctor arrived with Jonathan's update, I happily introduced these people as my family—and I meant it. Though my blood relatives lived across the Atlantic, these faithful friends refused to let me face this crisis alone.

After five stents and a prescribed medication regimen, Jonathan returned home following several days of care and extensive testing. He struggled with adjustment, as any pain triggered panic.

My Jonathan now faced his own trauma recovery. We partnered together through this—he helped me process my sexual trauma while I supported him through his panic attacks. Some doubted we would still relocate to America, but we recognized God's direction. We prayed for Jonathan's healing while maintaining our plans to move.

> **What you can do now:** During times of crisis while healing from trauma, create a "gratitude amid grief" practice. Each day, acknowledge both a difficult emotion and something for which you're grateful. This dual awareness helps prevent overwhelm from either extreme—toxic positivity or consuming darkness—and builds resilience by honoring your complete experience.

Embracing Freedom Beyond Religious Control

After Jonathan received medical clearance to travel—eleven weeks after his heart attack—we crossed the Atlantic once again with just our suitcases and bags. Our boys, now 15 and 17, accompanied us. Some belongings would follow by boat later.

The "Midwest group" subtly warned Jonathan that moving to the Carolinas instead of the Midwest would jeopardize our salvation. Jonathan ignored these controlling "voices" and followed God's direction. The cultish control over our spiritual welfare gradually disappeared as we developed a genuine relationship with God the Father. Following God's guidance brought security, knowing His presence remained with us. We watched the ties to the "group" dissolve one by one.

We settled smoothly with our friends and their church, who cared for us admirably and prepared opportunities for our missionary work. This became our focus as we established our new American life.

My oldest son enrolled into a college in Charlotte, North Carolina, while my youngest attended public school. We experienced many firsts. I'd never attended a football game—the "Midwest group" had forbidden it. I delighted in watching my youngest play, understanding only that the ball mattered. I cheered enthusiastically and prayed whenever helmets crashed. I purchased my first pair of trousers to stay warm at football games. Liberation had begun. We started living freely.

We enjoyed our United States life, experiencing previously forbidden activities. Our boys would live differently, breaking the cycle of cult control that Jonathan and I had endured. We escaped this environment, and our sons would never know it—they were spared. I'm profoundly grateful they never lived under the 'cultish' rules that Jonathan and I followed. Our entire family learned freedom together, enjoying life without legalism's constraints.

I rebuilt my music teaching studio for the third time and adapted to American life. We developed our missionary outreach, feeding orphans in Africa and raising funds for their care.

Physically, however, I deteriorated. Anxiety overwhelmed me. I lost weight rapidly and felt I was losing my mind. Though I'd experienced anxiety in England, this intensity surpassed anything previous. Darkness seemed to overshadow me. I desperately needed help. I prayed, quoted scripture, exercised—nothing brought relief. I didn't realize my body stored trauma. I merely survived rather than thrived. The situation terrified me.

Confronting Physical Manifestations of Trauma

I had no idea that what I was experiencing had a name, that researchers had been studying it for years. Childhood trauma doesn't just stay in your mind—it literally changes your body. The landmark Adverse Childhood Experiences Study discovered that people who experienced multiple traumatic events as children had dramatically higher rates of alcoholism, drug abuse, depression, and suicide attempts. They also faced increased health problems like chronic pain and illness.

Brain scans tell the story too. When trauma survivors are triggered, their fear center lights up like it's on fire while the rational thinking part of the brain goes dark. Your body genuinely believes the danger is happening again, right now. (Lanius et al, 2010)

This explained why untreated sexual trauma was destroying me physically. Therapist Allison Lieberman explains that the impact isn't just emotional—it's everywhere. Sleep, emotion regulation, relationships, physical health. The chronic stress weakens the immune system. And like so many survivors, I'd waited to seek help because of shame, fear of blame, and guilt.

Sexual trauma can manifest as internalized shame, PTSD, depression, gynecological problems, sexual disorders, eating disorders, low self-esteem, substance abuse, gastrointestinal issues, obsessive compulsive disorder, dissociative identity disorder, difficulty maintaining relationships, struggles with intimacy, and cardiovascular disease.

I hadn't realized my body had been keeping score all along, as trauma expert Bessel van der Kolk describes. My eating disorders with IBS, my racing heartbeat, the early morning dread, the obsessive thoughts of doom—my body was screaming for help.

Your stored trauma may manifest differently, but you aren't alone. You've begun the healing path. Recognize that abuse recovery takes time, whether years or days. You remain heard and seen. I'm here to walk alongside you as you discover your unique healing journey.

The physical manifestations of my trauma brought waves of silent grief that felt unbearable. This poem came from one of those darkest moments.

Silent Grief

Silent grief is debilitating, it zaps you like the lack of
electrolytes when your body has experienced intense
activity or illness.
You spiral, in a dizzy spin, no strength to soar high
above the grief.
It's dark, it's frightening, it's cold.
You come to a screeching halt, debating if you can or
will go forward.
You just can't cry anymore, like dry heaves when you
are very sick.
Then you look up, seeking guidance and direction
from the One that loves you the most.
He catches you as you spiral downward.
Like a bird, I have no strength to fly, I plunge to my death.
But Jesus catches me, I struggle, my wings just flapping,
He whispers as He holds me close, He whispers,
"Settle, just settle, I'm here".
He strokes my wings; they fold into my body.
He holds me close to His face.
I close my eyes, I settle.
I'm safe as He hums to me.
I have escaped death.

—Bridget Goodwin, 2021

Breaking the Stigma around Mental Health Treatment

Being the partner of a sexual abuse survivor presents
significant challenges. Jonathan struggled with intense
depression—hopelessness, silent withdrawal, lack of
motivation, and no desire to live. The cult-like mentality
instilled in us spoke negatively about seeking help outside

'the church.' The expectation was clear: if prayer or spiritual 'casting out' couldn't resolve an issue, you simply lived with it. We tried to support each other during this difficult period, but we desperately needed professional help.

The group twisted 2 Corinthians 12:7 to justify their position: *"a thorn was given me in the flesh, a messenger for Satan to harass me, to keep me from becoming conceited."*

By this logic, my depression, trauma, and mental health struggles existed to keep me humble. But when I actually read what Paul wrote in 2 Corinthians 12:8-9, I saw something different. He sought the Lord three times in prayer. God answered, saying, *"My grace is sufficient for you, for my power is made perfect in weakness."*

This was Paul's personal journey—not a template for my endless suffering. We can't use scripture to justify continued pain. Each person must seek God's direction individually. God will answer.

Mental health issues require proper attention. We must recognize depression symptoms courageously and seek appropriate help.

God uses various resources to facilitate healing. God's goodness stands in contrast to Satan's harassment of Paul. We seek the good God has planned—perhaps your healing involves relief from your 'thorn.' Your destiny may not require enduring needless suffering.

Jonathan needed professional assistance. Our sons encouraged him to consult a psychiatrist. Our boys played crucial roles in Jonathan's survival. We'd always maintained honest, authentic relationships with them. They witnessed our struggles and successes in England, where we relied completely on each other. During a particularly challenging period in the UK—with my trauma, our marriage struggles, and ministry pressures—I considered running away. Our boys pleaded with me to stay and work through our problems.

This survival journey included our sons' wisdom. Your healing path may differ, but find trusted family members or friends and listen to their insights. They may hold keys to unlocking your freedom.

We heeded our boys' advice, and I searched for a Christian psychiatrist. I found one specializing in veteran PTSD—perfect for Jonathan. Dr. B helped Jonathan and began addressing his depression. He asked Jonathan why he would take heart medication but resist brain medication. Jonathan found his healing source through talk therapy and medication. The process didn't end there—as Jonathan opened up, Dr. B clearly recognized I needed help too.

What you can do now: If you're hesitant about professional mental health treatment, write down the specific objections or fears holding you back. Next to each concern, write what might happen if that fear came true—and what might happen if you received effective treatment. This exercise helps clarify whether your hesitation stems from past conditioning or legitimate concerns, enabling more informed decisions about your healing journey.

Embracing Professional Diagnosis and Treatment

I witnessed Jonathan's relief through Dr. B's therapy and began searching for a female psychiatrist. Finding no suitable match, Jonathan encouraged me to see Dr. B. I resisted telling my detailed story to a man but took another brave step and scheduled my first appointment.

Dr. B approached me with gentleness and kindness. He listened attentively, giving me space and time to share my story. Though he never took notes during our sessions, he remembered every detail I shared. Each question revealed more clearly how awful and dreadful my experience truly was. Years of silence had sugar-coated the multiple levels of debauchery I'd kept hidden and locked away. Dr. B held his head in disbelief. The situation was severe—really severe.

A professional's viewpoint and diagnosis, founded on years of experience working with traumatized soldiers, provided clarity. His perspective broke through the deceptive voice Perseus had brainwashed me to believe. My situation represented evil and sin.

Dr. B diagnosed me with Complex-PTSD.

He prescribed medication. My brain required healing and rest. Initially, the medications made me feel shut down. I hadn't realized I constantly existed in a hyper aroused state—like a jet awaiting takeoff on a runway. I worried my creativity would disappear. Jonathan reassured me this adjustment would take time and encouraged patience. My brain needed calm and rest. Dr. B assigned homework: writing, running, outdoor time, and rest.

Grief struck again—how could I cope? Would I survive? Years lost, youth stolen. I was a sexual abuse victim in what should have been a safe place—my church—at the hands of my pastor. This was a cult.

When healing begins, you recognize how treacherous your trauma was. But you now have a starting point for climbing upward. You learn to release the past.

Trauma expert Diane Langberg explains: "Trauma always includes loss. The victim's sense of self is altered, as their way of functioning in this world. Trauma can dismantle faith and hope, and it turns what we thought was true upside down and backwards. Grieving their losses is grueling work."

Having faced my trauma's truth, what would I do with it?

Finding Expression Through Creative Healing

I allowed my poetry to chart my path through grief and sorrow. The anger and darkness that light revealed marked my healing journey.

As my sessions with Dr. B progressed, he suggested my healing would come through sharing my story. My mission field extended beyond feeding and clothing orphans in India and Africa—I needed to share my experience with women who had suffered similarly.

I argued with him, insisting I could never expose my past. Dr. B persisted, making storytelling part of my homework assignment.

When close friends discovered I was in therapy, they offered tremendous support. Unfortunately, many survivors face re-victimization when sharing their stories—a primary reason sexual trauma victims remain silent. They fear disbelief.

Research has identified several therapeutic approaches that proved effective for my healing journey. Trauma-focused cognitive behavioral therapy produces significant improvement in PTSD symptoms, with effects maintained over time.

Eye Movement Desensitization and Reprocessing, known as EMDR, has been found equally effective with large and stable treatment results.

For complex trauma specifically, phase-based treatment approaches show the most promise. These typically involve three stages: safety and stabilization, trauma processing, and integration with reconnection to ordinary life.

Research also confirms the therapeutic value of disclosure in safe environments. Sexual assault survivors who received positive social reactions upon disclosure showed better long-term adjustment and fewer PTSD symptoms than those who received negative reactions or didn't disclose at all.

Diane Langberg notes: "When you sit with one in overwhelming pain it will frighten you, and you will want to alleviate it quickly so both people in the room can feel better. Be careful. Pain is protest in the human constitution that something is wrong."

Offering a safe healing space through attentive listening was exactly what I needed. Langberg further observes: "In a survivor's healing, victims of abuse need to tell their story. They may be afraid, slow to speak, uncertain of their words. But as we listen, and bear witness to their trauma we grant them dignity, safety, and comfort. Doing so is a reversal of the experience of trauma."

Encouragement from close friends helped me reverse my trauma when they offered an opportunity to share my story at a music gathering. Three months into therapy with Dr. B, I recognized this would become part of my healing story. He shared experiences of patients whose trauma-sharing became progressively easier.

Could I take this step?

What you can do now: Explore different creative expression methods—writing, art, movement, music—to process emotions that feel too overwhelming for words. Spend 15 minutes daily with your chosen method without judging the result. This practice gives trauma a safe outlet when direct verbal processing feels too threatening, allowing your nervous system to discharge stored stress gradually.

Finding Strength to Share Your Truth

I asked Dr. B what to say when people questioned why I shared my story. He offered two options: blame him or admit I'd finally found the courage to come forward.

I chose the latter, sharing my story publicly for the first time after 40 years of silence and four months of therapy. As I approached the podium in a church filled with open, gracious, attentive people, I felt safe. This congregation knew how to support victims with love, and I felt their encouragement from where I stood. As I approached the podium, my husband unexpectedly joined me, taking my shaking hand and guiding me to sit rather than stand. He wanted to strengthen me through his presence while I shared my story. I'm deeply grateful for this safe haven.

My voice quivered, tears and makeup streaked my face, but I spoke. I shared my horrific story of loss and recovery—of redemption and hope in Jesus rather than vindication and justice. Even Dr. B questioned how I avoided becoming a 'hot mess.' I credited my faith. I began seeing God create something beautiful from this grotesque abuse narrative.

The experience liberated me, like being saved anew. The massive weight lifted. Friends commented on my changed countenance. I felt radiant in Jesus' liberating light.

Supporting Other Survivors in Their Journey

My exposed scars drew various responses. Some from the "Midwest group" probed painfully, asking, "Are you sure it was rape?" Yes—I was thirteen, and it happened on the pastor's office couch. I refused to hide anymore.

Others who had left the "Midwest group" showed me their scars, sharing how the same man had abused them in different ways, some similar to my experience. The discovery shocked me—I had no idea I wasn't alone! We formed a bond through our shared trauma. Phrases, encounters, events matched eerily—some victims had gone public previously (facing ridicule and disbelief), while others remained anonymous. All of us carried wounds. All had paid a high price for silence.

It became abundantly clear that church leadership had used cult-like power to abuse girls and boys, from sexual abuse to rape. This pattern trickled down to affairs between adults. Decades of abuse, infidelity, and deceit hid behind four-times-weekly church attendance.

The abuse pattern extended beyond the "Midwest group" to affiliated churches. In 2022, FBI agents investigated Florida churches, resulting in arrests and imprisonment of pastors and leaders awaiting trial. Though my abusers had died, I contacted the case detective and shared my story. I also shared with the prosecuting attorney representing the brave women who came forward.

Numbers provide strength, and shame drives sexual abuse victims into hiding. We must step into the light one by one, bringing hope to victims so they can begin healing.

We cannot tolerate or ignore this behavior. This is why I speak out.

Creating Safer Religious Communities

Church leadership positions demand proper safeguards—no exceptions. Appropriate tools exist to create safe churches. Churches must stop hiding abusers and re-victimizing those abused. Everyone in church ministry—from pastors to nursery workers—requires thorough vetting and investigation.

If only these measures had existed 40 years ago for me and countless other victims. I've carried this trauma's ramifications and will help others release their burdens. Rather than dwelling on 'what ifs' and 'whys,' we must stand up and speak out. By God's grace, I'll sound the alarm: 'Not on my watch!'

Churches have resources to learn safety protocols. I contacted NetGrace.org, an organization dedicated to empowering Christian communities to recognize, prevent, and respond to abuse.

NetGrace offers comprehensive safeguarding certification that includes expert training for every level of the church, help establishing a safeguarding team, on-site building risk assessments, and specific steps to create healing environments for survivors. Their team includes mental health experts, former prosecutors, and pastors with over 100 combined years addressing abuse-related issues.

This is exactly the kind of third-party accountability that could have prevented my abuse and protected countless other children.

To my dismay, the "Midwest Group" rejected this third-party investigation of my case. The institution that employed Perseus refused to acknowledge my years of sexual abuse and others' similar experiences. Their website video statements mentioned "someone" sharing abuse allegations, with their current pastor repeatedly using "if" more than ten times. They dismissed the situation saying, "he is dead so what can be done now?" This cover-up and support for my abuser re-victimized me. They continue promoting my abuser's messages, and people worldwide still admire him.

What you can do now: Research faith communities before joining by asking specific questions about their safety protocols. What training do staff receive? How do they screen volunteers? What reporting procedures exist? Do they have explicit policies about adult leader-youth interactions? Communities that welcome these questions typically prioritize safety; those that deflect may present higher risks for vulnerable members.

Focusing on Healing Rather Than Vengeance

I choose healing over revenge or retribution. Only God judges and will act justly. My mission focuses on helping those living with sexual trauma and church-inflicted harm. If my hurt, brokenness, and scars can help you, then my past suffering has purpose. This book aims to relieve you from past or present trauma and offer the hope I found in Jesus for healing. My healing path differs from yours, though similar threads may appear. We share one commonality—the God of strength, peace, and hope specializes in finding you where you are. No need to hide in darkness; Jesus approaches with beautiful rescuing light, gently drawing you out. Let God direct you as you courageously begin healing. Let me share what I've learned over the past two years: "This is not your fault."

Jesus wants to restore you piece by piece. Jesus offers healing balm for your scars. Jesus reminds you that you're beautiful, chosen, loved, and wanted. Jesus will help you love again.

Lessons Learned

Physical distance from toxic environments created the perspective I needed to see clearly. My move to England provided new surroundings where I could grow authentically. The cultural contrasts highlighted what hadn't been normal in my previous setting. This separation preceded my courage to question deeply ingrained beliefs and finally tell my truth.

I discovered that healthy ministry differs fundamentally from what I'd known. Genuine spiritual communities operate in ways I'd never experienced: true spiritual leadership empowers rather than controls, authentic community centers on people rather than buildings or institutions, genuine spiritual growth thrives without micromanagement, and service flows from love rather than obligation or fear.

In this healthier environment, my personal growth flourished—my education, new skills, and expanded horizons would have threatened the controlling structures of my past. The supportive relationship with Jonathan encouraged my development, helping me find my voice first in one area, then speaking the truth about my past. My growth would have posed a threat to those invested in my limitation.

Through Jonathan's loving response to my painful revelation, I learned that truth emerges in safe relationships. His genuine love created safety for my honesty. The secret lost its power when shared with someone trustworthy. His unconditional acceptance allowed buried truths to surface after decades of silence.

What initially felt like weakness—my vulnerability in sharing my story—became strength in the context of love. Taking the risk to be fully known led to deeper liberation, clearing the way for authentic connection in our marriage and setting the stage for healing that would continue to unfold in the years ahead.

What you can do now: If you recognize these patterns in your current church or religious community, consider reaching out to a professional who specializes in religious trauma recovery. Visit our workshop website at ihaveavoice.love to connect with others who have emerged from similar situations of spiritual abuse.

CHAPTER 10
The Healing Path

"If I can be a bridge spanning from my trauma to Jesus, and you would let me guide you to Jesus, then it has been worth it all."
– Bridget

†

As my therapist friend shared at one of my conferences, healing involves taking a step forward and sometimes two steps backward. That pattern defined my recovery. I can't emphasize this enough: healing shouldn't be rushed.

Whether you're clergy, someone who suspects abuse, or a survivor yourself, I'll guide you with the insights and awareness strategies I've learned along the way.

What is trauma?

Trauma is an emotional response to terrible events— accidents, crimes, natural disasters, physical or emotional abuse, neglect, violence (whether experienced or witnessed), losing loved ones, war, and more. Immediately after a traumatic event, shock and denial usually emerge.

Longer-term reactions include unpredictable emotions, flashbacks, strained relationships, and physical symptoms like headaches or nausea.

For me, trauma manifested in my stomach. I denied it for decades. When you experience trauma, your emotional distress can show up in your digestive system. My stomach problems began when I moved to the UK—my body craving healing while my emotions desperately needed stability. I had no idea my physical symptoms signaled deeper issues. I mistakenly attributed everything to IBS.

During my darkest moments of recovery, I wrote this poem to remind myself of my true identity—not as a victim, but as a warrior in training:

I'm Princess Warrior

I'm not broken, I'm not damaged goods I'm fierce
and strong.
At times when training, my strength is challenged,
I feel like saying, "I quit, I can't",
My trainer and the team around me, they will not let me.
"Come on P.W., you can do it!"
I reach for something inside that I do not believe
exists, strength.
I am really stronger than I could even imagine.
My spiritual journey challenges me as well.
My inner and outer strength is challenged.
Resistance builds muscles in your natural body.
Pressing against something makes you stronger.
I need others to surround me, to coach me so I do
not quit.
Reach for that inner strength of Jesus within you, the
power of His resurrection.
It is the good fight of faith; it is a battle.
He will supply my strength.
He is my sustenance, my portion.
He is training me for each battle,
My loved ones and friends are cheering me on.
I will win because Jesus has already won.
I am a Warrior, His Princess.

—Bridget Goodwin, 2021 & 2022

This poem became my battle cry when the healing journey
felt impossible. And I needed it, because understanding
trauma's grip on both body and mind would prove more
complex than I'd imagined.

Understanding and Responding to Trauma

When we talk about trauma, it's more than just a bad memory. It's an emotional response to a terrible event that completely overwhelms you. Your body and mind get caught in a storm they can't escape. I certainly felt that myself.

Here's what I've learned through both research and lived experience: trauma isn't just something that happens in your head. It triggers your body's threat response, releasing stress hormones designed to protect you. But when these hormones stay elevated for too long, they start breaking you down instead of building you up. Your internal alarm system gets stuck on high alert, wearing you out from the inside. This isn't 'just in your head'—it's physiological reality.

I've seen this pattern in countless survivors' stories, including my own. Research looking at multiple studies found that 70-80% of trauma survivors experience physical symptoms they don't even realize stem from their trauma (Afari, et al., 2014). Gastrointestinal issues, chronic pain, sleep disorders—these aren't random health problems. They're your body's way of holding onto memories your mind can't fully process.

Neuroscientists call this 'implicit memory'—how your body holds onto sensory trauma even when your conscious mind can't access it. You might feel something without understanding why. You carry a pain you can't explain.

For survivors and loved ones walking this healing journey together, understanding is the most important piece. Healing isn't a straight line. Current best practices in trauma recovery focus on truly seeing the person—understanding how common trauma actually is, recognizing its complex symptoms, responding with genuine compassion, and creating spaces that don't re-traumatize.

In my own journey, I've learned that trauma changes you. But it doesn't define you. Your body isn't your enemy. It's been trying to protect you all along.

What you can do now: Begin tracking physical sensations you experience during emotionally difficult moments. In a simple journal, note where you feel tension, pain, or discomfort in your body when triggered. This awareness helps establish the mind-body connection essential for comprehensive healing.

Now that you understand trauma's impact on body and mind, let's talk about how different people in your life can support your healing—and how you can support others walking this difficult path.

Perspectives in the Trauma Recovery Process

For Clergy: When someone in your care shows illness or unpredictable emotions, ask questions. Their approach to you demonstrates bravery because you've created safety. Simply ask if they've experienced harm, and allow them time to respond. Avoid touching them without permission. If praying for them, request permission to hold their hand. Never reach out without asking, and ensure you're not alone in a closed room. Think from their perspective and create safe interactions.

For Survivors: If you can't escape physical illness or relationship difficulties, take a break. Step away and document your feelings. Find a trusted confidant. What you're experiencing isn't 'all in your head'—you need support.

For Supporters: If you suspect someone experiences trauma aftermath, make yourself available. Simply be present without trying to fix them. Help them feel validated and valued through attentive listening. Acknowledge that while you may lack answers or diagnoses, you'll accompany them as they seek help. Most importantly, pray for them and provide space and safety.

While these feelings represent normal trauma responses, some people need additional support to move forward. That's where mental health professionals become essential partners in your healing journey.

What you can do now: Create a "safe person checklist" listing 5-7 qualities that make someone trustworthy for sharing painful experiences (examples: doesn't interrupt, maintains confidentiality, avoids minimizing feelings). Use this list to identify potential supporters in your healing journey.

Seeking Professional Support

My healing accelerated when I found a psychiatrist—another bold step away from the 'Midwest Group's' teaching against psychiatric analysis. Through research, I learned the differences between therapists, psychologists, and psychiatrists.

Therapists primarily listen and provide emotional coping tools through talk therapy. Psychologists typically hold advanced degrees with a therapeutic focus, combining counseling with psychological expertise. Psychiatrists, as medical doctors, can prescribe medication to coordinate brain and body healing alongside therapy.

Identify your intervention needs, name what troubles you, and address it directly. Though speaking with a stranger about deeply personal issues felt intimidating—knowing everything would be evaluated for diagnosis—I pushed forward.

I specifically chose a Christian psychiatrist who understood religious contexts and faith-based living. This approach helped me address both sexual trauma and church-related cult harm.

Your therapeutic path may differ—that's perfectly fine. Explore your options as I did. Pray about it, trusting God to guide you toward healing sources. Therapy illuminates suffering and establishes recovery paths. I believe God uses mental health professionals to help us thrive.

What you can do now: Research different mental health professionals in your area, focusing on those with trauma specialization. Create a comparison chart noting their approaches, costs, and whether they incorporate faith elements if that's important to you. Having this information organized makes taking the next step less overwhelming.

PTSD and C-PTSD

Both PTSD and C-PTSD result from experiencing deeply traumatic events, and they share key symptoms. People with either condition might struggle with flashbacks, nightmares, and insomnia. Both can make you feel intensely afraid and unsafe, even when the original danger has long passed.

But there's an important difference. Traditional PTSD typically results from a single traumatic event, while C-PTSD develops from long-lasting trauma that continues or repeats for months, even years. Think of it like the difference between surviving a sudden, intense storm and enduring a prolonged drought that slowly destroys everything around you.

C-PTSD was officially recognized in 2018 when it was added to the International Classification of Diseases. Research shows it typically develops from situations where escape is difficult or impossible—childhood abuse, domestic violence, or involvement in high-control groups like cults. These are my experiences.

While PTSD symptoms primarily cluster around fear responses to specific triggers, C-PTSD goes deeper.

It affects a person's entire sense of identity, emotional regulation, and ability to form healthy relationships. Studies have found that people with C-PTSD often experienced multiple types of trauma, longer exposure to traumatic experiences, and trauma that began earlier in life compared to those with traditional PTSD. Neuroimaging has even revealed more extensive changes in brain areas related to self-perception and emotional regulation.

The clinical distinctions matter because they point toward different healing approaches. But what matters most is this: whether your trauma came from one devastating event or years of accumulated harm, healing is possible. Your brain can rewire. Your body can find safety again.

The symptoms of C-PTSD extend beyond the fear-based responses of traditional PTSD. People with C-PTSD often struggle with what researchers call 'disturbances in self-organization'—difficulties with emotional regulation, negative self-concept, and problems in relationships.

In my own experience, I found myself caught in cycles I couldn't understand. My emotions would swing wildly, seemingly without reason. I felt fundamentally broken, as if the abuse had permanently damaged something essential in me. Relationships felt dangerous, even with people who genuinely cared about me. I'd push people away or cling too tightly, unable to find a healthy middle ground.

What you can do now: Create a symptom tracker where you can note which symptoms you experience and their severity on a 1-10 scale. This documentation helps you recognize patterns and provides valuable information for treatment professionals. Review weekly to identify progress and continuing challenges.

These weren't character flaws or spiritual failures, though that's what I'd been taught to believe. They were the predictable results of prolonged trauma, especially trauma that began in childhood when my sense of self was still forming. When you grow up in an environment where trust is violated repeatedly, where your reality is constantly questioned, where your needs are dismissed or punished— your brain adapts to survive that environment. Those adaptations make perfect sense in a traumatic situation, but they create problems when you're finally safe.

Understanding this changed everything for me. I wasn't broken or weak. My brain had done exactly what it needed to do to help me survive. Now I just needed to help it learn new patterns for this safer chapter of my life.

Management Strategies for PTSD & C-PTSD

Healing from PTSD isn't about finding a quick fix—it's about finding a way forward. Living with this condition doesn't mean your life is over. It means you're learning to navigate with courage and patience.

Professional treatment is crucial. Just like any serious health condition, PTSD requires dedicated care. But there's no one-size-fits-all approach. What works for one person might not work for another, and that's okay.

For those living with Complex PTSD, healing looks different. The symptoms go deeper than fear. They touch your entire sense of self—how you see yourself, how you connect with others, how you regulate emotions. It's not just about surviving a moment of terror, but about rebuilding an entire internal landscape that's been systematically dismantled.

Building a support system is everything. Not everyone will understand your journey, and that's painful. Some people might even re-victimize you through their misunderstanding. But there are those who will stand with you—family, friends, professionals who see your strength.

I found healing in unexpected places. Prayer became a lifeline. Journaling became a sanctuary. Poetry helped me process emotions too complex for simple words. My support group became my anchor—sometimes we prayed, sometimes we simply sat in understanding silence.

Self-care becomes a radical act of healing. It's more than bubble baths and positive affirmations. It's about creating safety—first internally, then externally. Some days, making your bed is a victory. Some days, taking a shower is an act of profound self-love.

Sleep matters more than most people realize. Anxiety loves the quiet darkness of night—that's when triggers can feel most overwhelming. Creating a safe nighttime routine, finding ways to calm your mind, these become essential practices.

Awareness is your first tool. Learn to listen to your body. Those moments of exhaustion, that mental fog, the unexpected surge of anxiety—they're not weaknesses. They're your body's way of communicating. Start keeping a journal. Not to analyze every moment, but to begin understanding your own language of healing.

Your healing won't be linear. Some days will feel impossible. Other days will bring unexpected joy. The goal isn't to eliminate every painful memory, but to create a life where those memories no longer control you.

Remember this: You are more than what happened to you. Your trauma is part of your story, but it is not the whole story. Healing is possible. Hope is real. And you—you are incredibly strong.

So, what does practical healing actually look like? Let me share the specific strategies that became my lifeline.

What you can do now: Choose one management or self-care strategy from this list that resonates with you and implement it for one week. Start small—even five minutes of deep breathing daily or writing down one negative thought and its healthier alternative can build powerful habits that support recovery.

My Personal Survival Manual for Trauma Recovery

My healing path included professional help from a licensed Christian psychiatrist specializing in psychiatric disorders and medication. Avoid self-diagnosis—seek help from specialists in your specific trauma. Whether you walk in faith, have recently begun serving Jesus, are considering accepting Jesus, or aren't religious at all, finding support remains critical. I chose a Christian psychiatrist, but your path may differ.

Whatever your choice, please seek professional assistance.

1. Talk Therapy & Medicine

I adhered to my talk therapy and medication plan for continued healing. After a year on brain medication, Dr. B gradually discontinued it, along with my sleep medication. I cannot emphasize enough the importance of continuing medication until your doctor determines otherwise.

Though the brain medication required adjustment time and initially made me feel numb and creativity-deprived, it helped my brain process memories and trauma. Medication may not be part of your solution—this represents my personal journey.

2. Running & Walking

Dr. B assigned homework including outdoor time doing activities I loved—particularly running. During my healing journey, I completed the Chicago Marathon and experienced my first runner's high. It was amazing!

There's research to support exercise in the healing journey. The physical and mental benefits of everything from gentle jogging to serious running are well known, and exercise—particularly running—can help reduce the symptoms of Post-Traumatic Stress Disorder (both PTSD and C-PTSD).

A University of Texas study found that people with PSTD who jogged for thirty minutes before therapy showed a greater reduction in symptoms than those who only attended therapy.

The reduction in symptoms comes from a boost in levels of a brain protein called brain-derived neurotrophic factor, or BDNF. This protein helps the brain adapt to stressors and repair itself, but it's generally low in people with PTSD or C-PTSD. It's also involved with learning and memory and plays a role in fear extinction by helping the brain establish context and, therefore, a sense of safety.

Studies showed that participants who exercised had increased levels of BDNF and became more receptive to therapy, which in turn helped reduce the severity of their PTSD and C-PTSD symptoms.

As PTSD UK shared from ultramarathon runner Joseph Miller, "Running is not a cure-all, but it continuously makes me better at dealing with PTSD, gives me the courage to face triggers, and the confidence that comes from facing a problem head on." (PTSD UK, 2019)

Numerous resources exist for physical activity tracking—downloadable apps, smartwatches, gyms, personal fitness coaches, or group sessions for those who thrive on competition. Get active!

Start walking, even just 1,000 steps daily—it's a beginning! I love using the Runkeeper app on my iPhone, which motivates me with five-minute progress updates. If you're feeling adventurous, try jogging, then increase to running. Always consult your doctor before beginning any physical activity.

3. Music

Music has provided tremendous solace through composing, singing, and playing piano.

Research shows that listening to your favorite music is a good way to escape the things that make you anxious and depressed—a much-needed distraction. But music as a therapy tool goes beyond that. It explores your responses to pieces of music to alleviate PTSD symptoms and relax you. This can include finding the best music to help you go to sleep quicker and have fewer nightmares.

So how does music therapy work?

One way music therapy affects mental health is that it stimulates the release of positive hormones such as oxytocin. One study found that people who sing for half an hour become energized and emotionally lifted by the experience, thanks to the rush of oxytocin.

Music also counteracts hormones linked to increased stress—particularly cortisol, the hormone that's often unregulated in people with PTSD. One study measured the drop in cortisol levels for individuals listening to soothing music in comparison to silence or rippling water. Music proved the most significant.

Setting aside the chemistry behind music therapy, it also provides sensory input that makes us instinctively ease muscle tension. This is why music is often used in conjunction with Progressive Muscle Relaxation.

I'd like to share a personal lullaby born during a particularly dark period. I began singing it spontaneously, with lyrics flowing naturally. During a night when anxiety awakened me—when demons typically attack through dreams, causing my heart to race and my sense of control to slip away—I felt myself shaking with racing thoughts. I began singing this newly composed song, which brought calm and peace, allowing me to fall back asleep.

The next day, while journaling, I realized God had given me a lullaby—a song to sing over me like a father comforting a frightened child awakened at night.

I'd love to share this with you for calming anxious thoughts:

Jesus, My All in All

Jesus, my Peace Giver,
Jesus, my Chain-breaker,
Jesus, my Deliverer,
Jesus, my all in all.

—Bridget Goodwin, 2018

What a beautiful reminder that whatever we need, Jesus is our all in all.

4. Writing Poetry

Capturing my recovery stages through poetry proved tremendously therapeutic. The complete emotional spectrum—grief, hatred, loss, anger, regrets, followed by glimmers of joy, love, mercy, and life-excitement—gradually filtered into my words.

I've included poetry throughout this book as a roadmap of my healing, emotional state, and recovery. I encourage you to document your thoughts. Sometimes writing comes easier than speaking—this begins your journey toward finding your voice, whether through pen or keyboard.

Many people have found that poetry serves as a core piece of therapy. For some, it's been their biggest way of understanding the world and their own experiences since childhood.

Poet Nicole Bouchard wrote on the healing powers of poetry: "Poetry can take the most extreme emotions and bottle them like tinctures that can be used to heal the reader; it is expression—giving a voice to that which we need as human beings to express, that gives poetry its strong influence."

Richard Gold describes a post on the Pongo site blog called "Poetry Saved My Life" (a line from a fourteen-year old's poem).

Gold says: "I've seen that life's worst experiences can exist as strangers in us, separate, like people we don't know and don't want to know. Yet these worst experiences remain our passionate life companions. I've seen that our emotions after life's worst experiences can be sealed in a variety of containers, some buried, or in a black hole, some that explode unexpectedly, some that exist only in the public realm, some that exist only in private, some that exist in one part of ourselves and not in others. But I've also seen that through poetry, people can open these containers, and move their contents, these painful emotions, into new frames that are more open and repurposed for a meaningful life."

Therapist Louis Hoffman describes three ways poetry helps his patients: Release, Processing Emotions, and Awareness and Insight.

He elaborates: "Poetry is often written during times when people are feeling intense emotions. In fact, the emotions often drive the poetry. Much like a good conversation or therapy session, poetry can provide a release... Poems often emerge in the midst of strong emotions. While part of what the poem does is describe the painful experience vividly and creatively, there's often a component of trying to make sense of the experience through understanding it more fully or through finding meaning in the suffering.

When this second component is part of the writing process or the reflections on the poem, it closely parallels therapy... Processing emotions often leads to greater self-awareness and new insights. There are many ways poetry can bring new insights."

5. Journaling

I found journaling with hand-drawn images immensely helpful while praying and meditating on scripture. This practice proved essential during periods of despair. Reading through my journal keeps me focused on the hope I've experienced through Jesus. Documenting fears on paper helps me face and release them. Reflecting on previous entries reveals my growth and unfolding recovery.

Writing about your most difficult experiences has surprising health benefits.

Dr. Susan Bali Hass shares: "When I was in medical school, a single lecture by a psychiatrist really impacted me. 'I give every patient two primary prescriptions,' he told us. 'Walk every day. Journal every day. You'd be amazed how much these two activities help one's mental health.' I never forgot it."

She continues: "I've always found journaling to be enjoyable and therapeutic. It's a profoundly helpful window into the behind-the-scenes workings of my mind, heart, and life. I recommend it to almost all my patients and coaching clients, particularly if they're feeling stuck or overwhelmed."

Research by James Pennebaker in the 1980s discovered a link between 'expressive writing'—writing for 15-20 minutes at a time, over several days, about a past traumatic event or secret concerns—and measurable improvements in immune system function. Doctor visits also decreased. These results have been replicated in patients with various conditions, including asthma, arthritis, breast cancer, and HIV.

Like poetry, journaling captures thoughts when you're not ready to verbalize your mental and emotional state. This becomes a mental journey tracking emotional waves and waning. I've followed my surges through peaks and depths. I've witnessed my healing and recovery progress. Seeing how good days gradually overtake bad ones proves encouraging. The writing process itself provides healing.

You might also use voice-to-text on your phone to capture thoughts if writing doesn't come naturally.

Start small, using your preferred style and approach. Release those thoughts from your head.

6. Strength Training

Long before seeking psychiatric help, I began weightlifting. I tapped into strength I hadn't believed I possessed. My personal trainer pushed me beyond fear-based limitations. I didn't realize God was establishing part of my recovery foundation through weight training.

Everyone knows that weight lifting increases physical strength. But for some, it can give psychological power too. Psychologists have long established that exercise is beneficial for mental health, and over the past decade, research has shown it can be a valuable tool for addressing post-traumatic stress disorder.

Despite weight lifting's associations with violent bursts of brawn, growing numbers of people who've experienced trauma are finding that pumping iron is a balm. For many, the sport's healing powers come down to this: where trauma has left them feeling helpless, powerless, and weak, lifting helps them feel strong—not only physically but also psychologically.

This happened to me—I felt empowered through physical strength. My trainer pushed me and called me 'P.W.,' Princess Warrior. I learned deadlifts, squats, leg presses, and bench presses. Despite initial terror, I learned to trust my trainer's gentle, safe coaching. He forbade me from saying, "I can't!"

About a year later, when I began therapy with Dr. B, prayer partners prayed for me as I struggled with reliving past memories and events. During this beautiful prayer time, someone said God called me His 'Warrior Princess.'

God winked at me—I already operated under this name, and He confirmed it. I'd developed physical strength and now learned to walk in His Spirit's empowerment as my physical body confronted mental weakness, pushing me toward greater strength.

What you can do now: Try progressive resistance training by starting with household items or bodyweight exercises. Begin with 10 wall push-ups, 10 chair squats, and 10 countertop rows three times weekly. Focus on the connection between building physical and emotional strength, gradually increasing resistance as you build confidence in your capabilities.

During one of my darkest periods, when the weight of healing felt overwhelming, I wrote the following poem. It reminded me that even when I felt most vulnerable, God remained my constant shelter through every storm.

Rock of Ages

You have been a rock through the ages for everyone.
You have been a constant for me, O Rock of Ages.
In the crevice of your Rock, I have felt very safe.
I have hid there in your shelter many times.
You have waited with me until the storm passed.
You have led me back down the path making sure
my foot does not slip.
Your radiant light guided me in the darkness until I
was on flat ground.
You spoke lovingly to me, "You must carry on. I am
with you every step of the way."
Every storm will pass, and I will rejoice with you in
the dancing sunbeams of light.
Until the next storm, I keep walking,
He will be my shelter.

—Bridget Goodwin, 2022

Supporting a Loved One with Trauma

Following Dr. B's advice alongside support from my family proved key to my survival. Learning how to guide and care for someone diagnosed with PTSD or C-PTSD is crucial, and resources exist to help.

My husband and sons supported me from the moment I shared my story. Their encouragement to seek therapy made my recovery possible. Here's something I need you to hear: victims shouldn't sacrifice their healing to 'protect' family members from painful truths. You don't need to carry that burden. I mention this because I carried it for years, which made me resist my psychiatrist's advice about sharing my story. You need family walking alongside you during healing.

If you're living with someone who has PTSD or C-PTSD, I know it's a trying condition. Living alongside someone in this battle can be complicated. But there are ways you can support and encourage your loved one.

First, become educated about the condition. Understanding what they're experiencing helps you respond with compassion rather than confusion. Be open to talking about the situation whenever they need it, but also offer space and time when they need that instead.

The balance isn't always easy to find, but your willingness to be flexible matters more than getting it perfect every time.

Encourage and assist them in scheduling and keeping therapy appointments. Sometimes the simple act of making the phone call or driving them to the appointment removes a barrier that feels insurmountable. Work to emphasize the need for healthy diet, sleep, and physical activity—not in a nagging way, but as someone who genuinely cares about their wellbeing. Consider attending treatment yourself to learn better ways to assist your loved one. This shows them they're not alone in this journey.

While no one has all the answers, there are practical things you can do to help. Accompany your loved one to doctor's visits when they want you there. Encourage them to maintain prescribed medications and counseling appointments without shaming them if they struggle. Show unconditional positive regard, compassion, and listening—these are worth more than any advice you could give.

In fact, avoid giving advice or making judgments. Your loved one needs a safe person, not another voice telling them what to do. Plan activities together that bring joy or peace. Give them space if they need it without taking it personally. Practice self-care and maintain boundaries that are healthy for you. And crucially, don't push them to tell you about their trauma. They'll share when and if they're ready.

The road is long, but your presence matters more than you know.

> **What you can do now:** If you're supporting someone with trauma, create a self-care plan that includes at least three activities you'll practice weekly. Supporting trauma survivors requires emotional stamina—you can't pour from an empty cup. Scheduling regular self-care ensures you maintain the strength to be present for your loved one.

As my healing progressed and I began to reconnect with joy, I wrote this poem on March 29, 2021. It captures a moment of breakthrough—recognizing that transformation through Christ brings not just survival, but celebration.

A Dance in Your Step

There's something that happens when you accept the
Lord as your Savior.
You are filled with His Spirit.
You are transformed.
You have a dance in your step.
A song in your heart.
A new beginning is yours.
Those that have been walking this way for many
years still need to be replenished.
A saturation of His Spirit is never withheld.
It is for the new born and the veteran.
At times we all need to be reminded why there's a
dance in a child of God's step,
A song in our heart,
We are children of the King!
We are redeemed!
We have eternal life!
His blood paid it all!

—Bridget Goodwin, 2021

Rewiring Your Mind with Truth

At one of my conferences, my keynote speaker, a certified neurocoach, shared about the "rewiring of our brain" through the brain science of healing. You take the lies told to you by your abuser and replace them with truths.

Romans 12:2 speaks powerfully to this process:

"Do not be conformed to this world, but be transformed by the renewal of your mind, that by testing you may discern what is the will of God, what is good and acceptable and perfect."

As my keynote speaker explained, you place the lies told to you on trial, addressing them one by one, and replace them with truth.

Jesus emphasized this transformative power in John 8:31:

"If you abide in my word, you are truly my disciples, and you will know the truth, and the truth will set you free."

This process of replacing lies with truth isn't something that happens overnight. It's daily work, ongoing work. Even now, years into my healing journey, I still wrestle with some of those old lies trying to creep back in.

Living with Complex-PTSD: My Ongoing Journey

Here's what I want you to understand: healing doesn't mean you're suddenly fixed and everything is perfect. It means you're learning to live with what happened while refusing to let it define your future. Some things I still navigate as someone with Complex-PTSD include:

Forgiveness takes time—I'm still working on it, and that's okay. Getting lost makes me afraid because the loss of control triggers something deep. Yelling makes me scared, no matter who's doing it or why.

I have to actively shake off the doubt and doom, the feeling that something dreadful is going to happen.

I still deal with anxiety, but I'm learning how to cope with it. My mind still races when I wake up in the middle of the night, but I'm learning how to calm the voices of lies. At times I sing my lullaby, "Jesus, My All in All", or I quote a scripture I have memorized: *"I have set the Lord always before me, because He is at my right hand, I shall not be shaken."* (Psalm 16:8)

I still face the fear that I will be rejected and not believed. I feel the weight of my burden on my husband, who gladly carries my baggage as I heal. I still have horrific dreams. It's a survival of everyday, but I celebrate the glimmers—those small moments of light and hope.

I must take time to pray and read God's Word or I start to withdraw inwardly.

Without God and all of His provisions, I would not continue to heal.

I can't change the past, which is why I try so hard in the present.

When I see a 13-year-old girl, I compare my life to hers and long for a chance to start over.

If I shut down and withdraw, it's because of my trauma, but I'm trying to overcome that—be patient with me.

I'm learning to trust again. I hate confrontation, but I'm trying to be bold and stand up for myself.

I fight the voices that tell me the impending judgment of God is going to strike me down. I've replaced those voices with truth: God loves me as His daughter. He will perform in my life His goodness—it will chase me down, just as my father would love and shower me with good things.

Finding Your Support Team: You Need Pacers

This ongoing journey isn't meant to be walked alone. As you start your healing journey, you'll create your own handbook of survival. Give yourself grace, time to reflect, and be renewed. You must surround yourself with support.

When I ran the Chicago Marathon, I found myself with a group of pacers. I ran with them and felt the drive from the group that I could do what they were doing. It became a moment of enlightenment for me. To succeed in my Christian walk, I need pacers to cheer me on, with like-minded goals. Alone, it can be done, but the struggle holds one back. In a group, you're empowered and compelled to keep going.

Find your pacers and let them cheer you on: "You can do it!" Life will get better, and you can be restored.

I'm cheering for you!

Lessons I've Learned Through Healing

Through my journey of trauma and healing, I've discovered that recovery rarely follows the path we expect. For me, it began with physical symptoms I couldn't explain, followed by the painful excavation of memories I'd buried for decades.

When I awakened to the reality of my abuse, profound grief followed—anger, confusion, and sorrow for my stolen innocence and lost opportunities. These emotions weren't wrong. They prepared the ground where healing could finally take root. My journal, poetry, and therapy sessions became sanctuaries where I could process these emotions honestly until I was ready to move forward.

Professional help proved essential; despite everything I'd been taught about relying solely on faith. I believe God uses various sources to partner with our faith, strengthening it as we see Him intervene and work through others to facilitate our healing.

Dr. B's compassionate guidance, combined with medical intervention, gave me tools I never knew existed. Each step toward health—from that first terrifying appointment to sharing my story publicly—required courage I didn't know I possessed. My family's unwavering support, physical activities that reconnected me with my body, and creative expression through music and writing became channels for restoration. Wholeness itself became an act of resilience against darkness.

Though my journey began with tears and physical illness, it has blossomed into a life more meaningful than I could have imagined. This is evidence that new beginnings await anyone brave enough to step through healing's open door.

CHAPTER 11

What's Next

"Let me sound the alarm to keep you from harm." – Bridget

†

My sexual trauma was hidden by my church trauma. The cultish environment of my old church in the Midwest allowed the trauma to occur and reoccur. I shared with you the characteristics of cults in chapter six.

In this chapter, I want to share some essential warning signs of clergy abuse based on my experience with that church because knowing these patterns can help you recognize danger and prevent future harm.

Recognizing Religious Authority Abuse

Religious abuse often shows the same red flags, no matter the religion. Spiritual abuse involves spiritual leaders using their power to control, which often leaves their victims both hurt and spiritually confused that this abuse was allowed to happen by God (Oakley & Kinmond (2013).

And abuse by religious leaders is especially harmful. A study looked at 186 people who had been abused and found it not only damages your trust in the abuser, it also damages your faith in God and the church (Pellauer, et al, 2018). Their research showed that victims often experience what theologians' term 'religious trauma syndrome,' with symptoms similar to PTSD but specifically related to religious experiences.

The Diana Garland Center's landmark study (Garland & Argueta, 2010) found that about 3.1% of women who regularly attend religious services experienced clergy sexual misconduct. The pattern of this abuse includes: gradual boundary-pushing, religious language used to excuse it, and isolating victims from those who might help them.

The most effective prevention strategies involve systemic approaches: clear policies about appropriate boundaries, regular training for all church personnel, and established reporting mechanisms that don't funnel through a single authority figure (Rudolfsson & Tidefors, 2015).

What's most troubling is that institutions often protect themselves, not victims. (Fortune & Poling, 2020). This is both startling and terrifying, but we can learn and watch for the signs.

My heart has been overwhelmed by all the damage of religious and sexual abuse that has happened or is still happening in church communities all around the world that should be places of protection. I have prayed for you, and I'm your advocate. The poem below reflects my heart for you, for your healing and restoration.

I List Your Names in Prayer

I list your names in prayer today,
I speak your name, listing each one of you.
We share the same story, we have been abused, sexually.
I cry as I write this, we have a common bond,
But I'm determined that this will not remain as a
horrific memory,
But a message of hope, seeking Jesus to heal you
beyond your wildest dreams.
We have learned to hide our many, ugly scars, but as
we heal, we realize that these scars do not define us.
We are not these scars; we are not what our abusers said!
We are loved, we are special, we are unique because
JESUS has saved us!
We did nothing to deserve abuse, we were victims.
We rise above and we are becoming victors.
We learn to not hide our scars, because we want to
prevent others from succumbing to them.
We learn to speak about our scars without shame,
because we want others to know they are not alone.
We declare hope, because Jesus is ever present, a
light to shine in the deepest, darkest valley or caverns
of our heart.
The darkness must submit to His ray of hope.
I will encourage you, pray for you, and reach out my
hand to you.
You may not be ready to share your story, and you
may be embarrassed of your scars, that's ok.
I'm praying for you; Jesus is the only answer.
HE is our hope.

—Bridget Goodwin, 2021

Seven Critical Signs of Spiritual Abuse

Years after I escaped, I discovered the work of abuse recovery specialist Marquette Smith. Reading her description of spiritual abuse patterns, I felt seen for the first time. Everything I'd experienced—everything I'd been told was normal, godly, right—suddenly had a name. The framework she outlined in "7 Signs of Spiritual Abuse" helped me understand what had happened to me and gave me language to help other survivors recognize these patterns.

Ken Blue writes in *Healing Spiritual Abuse* that just as physical abuse means someone exercises physical power over another causing physical wounds, and sexual abuse means someone exercises sexual power causing sexual wounds, spiritual abuse happens when a leader with spiritual authority uses that authority to coerce, control, or exploit a follower, causing spiritual wounds.

David Johnson and Jeff Van Vonderen describe it this way in *The Subtle Power of Spiritual Abuse*: spiritual abuse occurs when a leader uses their spiritual position to control or dominate another person, overriding feelings and opinions without regard for that person's well-being. Power is used to bolster the leader's position and needs above the person seeking help.

I lived this. I know these wounds. And I've learned to recognize the warning signs.

1. God Syndrome

The leader claims to be God's exclusive messenger, insisting that God speaks only through them and that following them equals following Jesus. In my experience, these leaders are often emotionally unstable, switching between charm and criticism without warning.

Perseus told his congregants that his ministry was to the elite attainers of the Kingdom and that this was the vehicle to the Kingdom of God. He said he would slow down his walk with Jesus so we could follow him—not Jesus directly, but him. Right before his death, he announced his plan in one of his last messages: "Anyone who is not completely confident that I'm God's man, and whose undying allegiance and loyalty is not to me, will no longer have a position on our church staff or live on our church property."

Several people left after this. Many others remained. The man's influence over the people was powerful. After thirty years of leadership, he still needed to threaten people to follow him without question. We thought he was being humble by slowing down for us. We couldn't see that he'd placed himself between us and Jesus.

2. Pulpit Idolatry

The leader demands not just respect, but actual worship. They create elaborate entrance rituals, require standing ovations, and punish anyone who doesn't show sufficient reverence.

Perseus always made a grand entrance right before service started. He entered from the back of the congregation and walked up to the platform, nodding and smiling to those he chose. If he acknowledged you, that made you special.

When he left at night in his big blue Cadillac, the head usher and a group of young men walked behind his car in a grand procession until he pulled onto the street. All of us waited in the hallway to say goodbye and walked out to the sidewalk to wave. We treated him like he was the President. Looking back, I see how this elevated him to a position that belonged only to Jesus.

3. Burned Out and Exhausted

The abusive leader creates an exhaustion that goes far beyond normal church involvement. You're told that "church work is first, and everything else comes second." You're made to feel guilty for not serving or taking a break from your ministry. You're trapped in a project-driven church where the leader forces you to participate in multiple projects with little to no breaks in between—forgetting that even God rested on the seventh day.

So many of my nights were occupied with church activities. We invested countless hours of our personal lives into church work and various projects. You served and wore this badge of honor by showing up. Cleaning, band practice, church services three times a week, volunteering at the church school during the day, and any other extra activities filled our schedules.

Our weekends centered around church—Saturday night, Sunday afternoon, and Sunday evenings. Family always took a back seat; the church came first. Many missed family functions because they conflicted with church attendance. You were noticed by your presence, not your absence. Family life suffered, but we were told to put the church first and God would save our children and family.

4. Perfectionism and Rigid Rules

The leader requires you to follow super strict rules to prove you're "purified" and "cleaned" to serve. You're told you must be totally mature before serving the Lord. But really, they want total submission before you can be trusted in any ministry. The leader hopes you'll become so brainwashed with rigid rules that you'll never step out of line.

Since I played in the church band, I had to prove I was worthy to participate. We followed a list of rules, and breaking them meant being "kicked out of the band." One rule required testifying at least once every month. Another prohibited wearing trousers, earrings, or any "ungodly" clothing. If you visited an amusement park, you could no longer participate in the band. We constantly had to prove we were "purified and cleaned to serve in the church."

5. Stripped Individualism and Controlling Private Life

The leader makes rules that control every single move you make outside of church. I'm not talking about basic Christian teachings, but how leaders twist those teachings to control every part of your life. You get programmed to act, talk, and respond to life exactly how the leader sees things.

Every life decision—dating, jobs, even buying a car—required consultation with Perseus. Any individuality faced banning and ridicule. Those who didn't seek his counsel for decisions were labeled rebellious. We were brainwashed to believe he spoke for God. Sometimes his advice worked; other times it created disaster.

Even the color of a car carried moral implications. The color red was deemed inappropriate—no child of God would drive a red car, especially not a pastor.

Ironically, while pastoring in England, my husband and I needed a car but couldn't afford one. God provided through someone we'd just met who felt divinely prompted to give us his car. What color was it? Red!

God can't be constrained by arbitrary rules. He created the red rose, the red robin, the red ruby, red strawberries, the red fox, the red Irish setter, and painted one stripe of the rainbow red. While humans may associate red with evil, it's also the color of redemption—the color of Jesus's blood shed for our salvation.

6. Fear-Based Control

The leader uses fear and bullying to control people, creating a suffocating fear that keeps followers depending on them for all of life's answers. They don't welcome individual ideas. Instead, they use a terrifying fear of "the enemy" (the devil). You'll notice the leader constantly talks about the enemy and what the enemy is doing.

More emphasis is placed on fighting dark forces, leaving people scared of the spiritual world. Paranoia takes over, and followers become totally dependent on the leader to show them how to live in the scary world the leader has created.

Another quote from Perseus's pulpit message: "God didn't stand a seducing spirit but he stood a power of the world to come behind this pulpit, someone to be submitted to, someone to be respected." This created fear that we must listen to the future leader of the Kingdom of heaven.

In reality, he programmed us to look to him rather than Jesus, the author of our faith. Only through Jesus can we be saved. Jesus is the head of His church.

"And he is before all things, and in him all things hold together. And he is the head of the body, the church. He is the beginning, the firstborn from the dead, that in everything he might be preeminent." (Colossians 1:17-18, ESV)

7. Island Mentality

The leader acts like their church is the only church that hears from God. They claim they alone have the truth and practice the only real Biblical Christianity. They speak against other churches and constantly compare their church to others. Whether they do this openly or secretly, it's clear to followers that "our Church" has everything and they should never venture outside.

If followers leave, they get talked about publicly and made to feel like they've rejected God. The message is that something terrible will happen to them or that God will punish them for leaving.

In my personal sexual trauma experience, Perseus's control dominated my daily life. I had to be perfect, even taking thyroid pills to keep my body thin. I was a trophy to be displayed. He selected my finest clothes, down to my shoes. Somewhere behind this beautiful facade, I was hidden. I lived in constant fear of discovery. If I failed to meet his standards, he humiliated me, claiming that my looks and behavior invited flirtation from men. This was my pastor! This behavior stood in stark contrast to Jesus's love.

As church members, we were told we belonged to the only true church in the city. In reality, our city contained many churches with people faithfully serving God and the community. We never engaged in community service. We remained isolated because we considered ourselves God's select group. The truth had supposedly been revealed exclusively to our leader, who preached under divine direction. I remember walking door-to-door distributing church brochures, terrified someone might recognize Perseus from his visits to my neighborhood home. The fear was paralyzing!

The Contrast: True Leadership vs. Cult Leadership

God embodies love, compassion, truth, mercy, and grace. He demonstrates patience and long-suffering. Shouldn't spiritual leaders follow God's example in loving His people?

We could have become a powerful force serving our community if equipped with love, compassion, and truth—the natural results of walking with Jesus. Instead of reflecting His servant leadership, the cult leader focused entirely on self-promotion. Jesus entered Jerusalem not on a majestic stallion with trumpets heralding His arrival, but on a humble donkey, met by crowds crying "Save us!" (Hosanna!).

True leadership serves and gives. Cult leadership consumes and takes.

If you or someone you know experiences any of these seven signs of spiritual abuse—run! Like other forms of abuse, spiritual abuse causes devastating, long-lasting effects. Consider what steps you need to take to escape and find a loving church full of compassion and truth.

Churches should provide safe havens, directing people to God, the author and finisher of our salvation. Jesus is the only way to salvation. If anyone claims you need them to reach heaven, flee immediately. A true leader walks beside you as a fellow disciple of Christ, helping you build a stronger relationship with Jesus—not with themselves.

You must declare your truth to heal, and the next poem reminds us that Jesus is our Truth!

Speaking Truth

Today as I awakened, anxiety was at my window of
my soul.
I refused to open that window.
Unlike a closed door, I could see what was waiting for me.
That old familiar face of fear, dread and turmoil it
was staring at me.
No, I will not succumb to you.
I choose to be thankful instead.
I whisper a declaration of gratitude through prayer.
It may be a whisper, but I'm still speaking.
I will speak my truth even if my voice shakes, and my
legs wobble.
I feel unstable, but I know I'm still healing.
I will speak my truth even if my soul is still crying.
My truth is Jesus.
My healer is Jesus.
Jesus walks with me, I sense His presence.
He rescued me, delivered me.
My cage was demolished.
My chains destroyed.
My scars show, 43 years of bondage leaves its mark.
Jesus has healing oil for me.
You may see my scars, and poke at them to see if
they are real.
You may not understand why I'm not over it.
You may think I'm not walking in victory but I'm
walking with Jesus, and that is my victory.

—Bridget Goodwin, 2023

Finding a Healthy Faith Community

Through my journey with God, I've realized He created the family unit first—Adam, then Eve as his companion. This established the natural order from creation's beginning. The church should function as a community strengthening both young and old, married and single.

It should provide a safe haven for sharing God's Word and corporate worship, where individual gifts develop and flourish. Whether visiting the elderly or serving in other ways, the church connects people with opportunities that allow their gifts to thrive through service.

I loved being part of church plants while pastoring in England with my husband. I enjoyed discovering each member's strengths and walking alongside those working through weaknesses. Building a church requires balancing labor and love. Initially, we focused too much on the building itself, but God showed us the people matter most.

I've seen both approaches: extreme allegiance to the church building that placed family second (which sometimes worked but bred bitterness) and prioritizing family with church activities supporting family time (which created healthy, joyful communities).

You can find a healthy church that loves Jesus and your family—one offering activities for all ages and opportunities to help local and global communities. I've found such a place after spending almost a year without a church home. I struggled to belong in a mega-church where I remained just a visitor.

While I enjoyed visiting other churches with good music and preaching, I didn't feel I belonged. Then this church found me when I started working there. I gained a welcoming, loving community that needed me as much as I needed them. My pastor points me to Jesus and Scripture, prays for me, and creates safety. He respects my family time rather than demanding my constant presence—a refreshing change from my past experience.

Taking a break from church attendance is okay. Listening to services online is okay. Setting boundaries is okay. When the time feels right, you'll find your people, your community, your church home. You don't need a church for salvation—you need Jesus—but a healthy church helps strengthen your walk with Him.

You weren't designed to walk this journey alone. Let Jesus guide you. You are loved and valued. Never stop praying; God sees and hears you.

My mission is for you to be rescued.

Resources for Help
- Christianpsychological.org
- Netgrace.org
- Choosingtherapy.com
- Rainn.org
- Clergysexualmisconduct.com
- Restoredvoicescollective.com
- Healthline.com
- Safeharborim.com
- Ncadv.org

What is My Mission Field?

You are my mission field.
Your salvation and relationship with Christ are worth
more than pearls, rubies or gold. This was purchased
with His crimson blood.
If my story prevents you from being lost in this abyss
of guilt and shame, then my mission has been worth it.
Your virtue, your peace of mind, your freedom, your
voice being heard, this will become your testimony.
What is that testimony?
You are valued, and Jesus loves you, right where you are!
You can be saved, you can be forgiven, you can make
it, you can carry on, you can be restored!
You have already been ransomed, redeemed by the
price of the spotless Lamb of God!
You will rise up, a miracle like me, and you will be
brave, you will save others through the word of your
testimony of Jesus!
Go forth my daughter, my sister, my brother, my
son, you are chosen, you are special, special to the
Father, your Heavenly Father.

—Bridget Goodwin, 2021

You are valued, and you are worth going after. You deserve
to be saved. No more darkness for you.

Out of the Darkness and Into the Light

Come out of the darkness and into His Light.
Darkness has been enveloped, swallowed by Jesus'
redeeming light.
He broke through my darkest night and banished all
lurking shadows.
This trail of tears has been replaced with redeeming
tears of love and joy.
This path of healing is illuminated with His Glory.
Jesus wants me to be His glory light bearer.
Jesus' powerful power of Glory wants to partner with
me, with you!
Taking back what the enemy stole with other glory
bearers!
Redeeming love that sets the captive free, holding
this glorious torch that is full of His Power.
It will swallow the darkness and invade the camp of
the enemy
We will take back the plunder that has been left
behind by the enemy with restoration and redemption,
A place that is better than a victim can ever imagine.
A place of healing and illumination.
What was left in the heap of ashes,
Jesus is going to transform that to beauty.
What was left of the dry, parched soul of loneliness,
confusion and shame is going to be healed with the
oil of anointing.
Every broken heart that has been cloaked in grave
clothes, these garments of death,
Will be disintegrated in the flame of His power, of
His glory. You will dance with joy and gladness
You will be strong, no longer feeble like a twig that
breaks under resistance.
You will become a grand, majestic oak planted by His
River of restoration.
This River that you have now immersed yourself
into, it becomes everything to you, where you are

baptized, restored, and refreshed.
Your roots are grounded in this vast River that supplies.
You will grow, no longer dwarfed, cut back, and withered.
You now can be commissioned for your mandate,
saturated in His love, and glory,
To be His glory bearer and go to those places to
recover the ones that are trapped.
Let's go into the caves and rescue those imprisoned
in the darkness of their shame and secrecy.
I will hold your hand; we will hold your hand.
Jesus holds our hand, and that hand is safely in the
father Abba, our Papa.
We will go forth in the hope of His glory, my
Redeemer, my Savior, my Jesus.

—Bridget Goodwin, 2024

Lessons Learned

Through my journey from spiritual captivity to freedom, I've discovered that healthy faith communities look fundamentally different from what I experienced for decades. True spiritual leaders point to Jesus rather than themselves, respect family boundaries, and create

environments where questions and growth flourish. They collaborate rather than control, remain accountable to others, serve humbly, and emphasize grace instead of fear. The contrast between my past experience and authentic spiritual leadership couldn't be more stark—one imprisoned while the other liberates.

Speaking out about abuse creates protection for others, and I've embraced this advocacy as part of my healing journey. Your story, like mine, can prevent others from experiencing similar trauma. I've learned that warning signs become clearer in hindsight, but sharing them helps others recognize danger before abuse occurs. Every safety measure shared, every red flag identified, and every boundary suggested saves lives. While my voice once trembled when speaking truth, I now see my story as a bridge spanning from trauma to healing that others can cross to find their own freedom.

Finding community after abuse takes time and patience. I needed almost a year without church attendance before finding a healthy congregation. Online resources, supportive friends, and professional help bridged this gap. If you're struggling to trust religious communities again, know that healthy ones exist—but taking breaks, setting boundaries, and healing at your own pace is essential. True faith always empowers rather than controls, bringing freedom rather than bondage. Jesus modeled servant leadership, not dominance,

and authentic spirituality thrives in environments of honesty, safety, and grace. Your journey toward healing happens best in community, but only when that community reflects Christ's love rather than human control.

Taking Action to Protect Yourself and Others

If you find yourself, or witness someone else, experiencing these warning signs, please seek help immediately. Tell the truth to someone you trust, find a support group, report it to the proper authorities, and get professional counseling.

Let's be light bearers who expose evil and call it out.

Let's link arms with fellow survivors who refuse to allow this to continue, sounding the alarm together.

Let there be no more harm!

Essential Safety Measures for Prevention

1. Maintain open communication channels. Never let anyone become isolated to where they must keep secrets out of fear. Ensure your loved ones can speak freely with you or family members. Nothing is too trivial or too serious to discuss.
2. Establish a "no secrets" policy. No secrets with your loved ones or family members—NO EXCEPTIONS.
3. Seek help when truth becomes distorted. If truth has been perverted, seek help to uncover reality.
4. Recognize predator patterns. Perpetrators target vulnerable, quiet individuals. Warn your children that any special attention should be shared with you, no matter how innocent it might seem.
5. Stay vigilant. When you've experienced abuse, you develop vigilance to prevent recurrence. Even without personal experience, you can remain alert and protective.

You might save someone from years of damage and recovery—a beautiful gift of protection.

Chapter 12

My Encounter with Forgiveness

"My transformation is a beautiful thing, taking the void and revealing colors that you can only imagine as I'm engulfed in the light of the Son." –Bridget

†

You'll find well-meaning people who, upon learning you're healing from sexual trauma, will give you pointers on forgiveness. I've heard them all and you likely will, too. When I was learning to forgive, I realized my relationship with Jesus needed to reflect transformation in my life. When you encounter Jesus, you're never the same. You change as you mirror Him, His love, mercy, and forgiveness.

I couldn't forgive. I knew I should; the Holy Bible mentions forgiveness in various forms approximately 126 times, and the word 'forgive' appears about 23 times in the New Testament. Here are a few passages that have always stuck with me:

"Then Peter came up and said to him, 'Lord, how often will my brother sin against me, and I forgive him? As many as seven times?' Jesus said to him, 'I do not say to you seven times, but seventy-seven times." (Matthew 18:21-22 ESV)

How could I forgive when invasive thoughts assaulted me dozens of times daily?

"For if you forgive others their trespasses, your heavenly Father will also forgive you, but if you do not forgive others their trespasses, neither will your Father forgive your trespasses." (Matthew 6:14-15 ESV)

And: *"Blessed are the merciful, for they shall receive mercy."* (Matthew 5:7 ESV)

How could I show mercy when hatred burned so strongly within me?

How could I be a follower of Jesus and *not* forgive my abuser?

My Heavenly Father had the answer, and I needed to discover it through forgiveness—a lesson learned by forgiving. It happens inside the heart, in the deepest part of the soul. The place that was injured needs healing, and it must begin with forgiveness.

But that doesn't mean it's *easy*.

Understanding True Forgiveness After Trauma

Research distinguishes between different types of forgiveness. In the work of Enright & Fitzgibbons (2015), decisional forgiveness involves choosing not to be unforgiving, and emotional forgiveness involves replacing negative emotions with positive ones. Research suggests that trauma survivors sometimes decide to forgive before they actually feel it.

Importantly, research consistently shows that forgiveness helps the survivor, not the person who caused the harm.

Forgiveness is for *us*, not *them*. And in fact, a meta-analysis of 54 forgiveness studies found that our choice to forgive significantly improves our mental health—specifically helping us heal from depression, anxiety, and post-traumatic symptoms (Wade, et al., 2014).

Therapeutic forgiveness doesn't need you to reconcile with the abuser, excuse or minimize the harm, forgo justice or accountability, or just let go of the emotional pain.

Instead, forgiveness in trauma recovery means a gradual release of the emotional burden that keeps survivors tethered to their abusers (Herman, 2015). The timing of forgiveness work is crucial, too; trying to forgive too early in trauma treatment can be harmful, but when the time is right for the survivor, the act of forgiving—sometimes over and over—can lead to deeper healing (Worthington & Langberg, 2012).

Forgiveness and mercy are part of Jesus's divine nature. On the cross with His body wrecked and gravity pulling His weight against the nails that held Him up, Jesus took time to talk with the man on the cross beside Him. Jesus worked to save the lost until His last breath. What did He say to this criminal who asked to be remembered when Jesus came to His Kingdom?

"Truly, I say to you, today you will be with me in paradise." (Luke 23:43 ESV)

Such love and mercy I witnessed from my Savior. He began preparing my heart to forgive. He spoke so lovingly to me that I knew I must speak in love and mercy. To love like Jesus isn't easy, but He gives us power to overcome every obstacle.

When I first shared my testimony, I openly admitted I hadn't forgiven Perseus. My close friends and loved ones knew I couldn't forgive him—not yet. And some judged me for that, while others showed compassion. When I reached out to NetGrace.org, the counselor who spoke to me was incredibly kind. He told me not to carry this heavy burden of unforgiveness. Jesus would take this burden away for me.

What you can do now: Create a "forgiveness inventory" by listing people associated with your trauma experience. Don't pressure yourself to forgive immediately, but acknowledge where you are in the process with each person. This awareness is the first step toward emotional freedom.

Experiencing the Transformation That Sets You Free

I attended a Women's Conference and came home transformed. This is why I believe it's so imperative to your healing that you attend women's conferences and workshops where others can pour into you. And, ultimately, it's why I founded I Have a Voice Ministries—to help women and even men encounter Jesus and be transformed. (If you would like to join the next conference, visit: www.ihaveavoice.love.) And through this Ministry, my mission is to host meetings and workshops each year that give voice to the silenced, so that everyone who has experienced the pain of abuse can one day feel the joy of healing.

The word that spoke to me that weekend at the Women's Conference in Mississippi was 'forgive.' Many informative and enlightening words were spoken by women who had experienced sexual abuse. These words pierced my heart and went straight to the core of my unforgiveness.

So much had happened in my life on my journey of healing and being set free by finding my voice, but it remained muffled. Now it was time for me to forgive my abuser and speak to be heard.

How could I help others unless my own heart was free? Complete freedom was what I needed. It needed to be unlocked, and another key was required.

Mrs. Gentle One walked me through the steps of forgiveness. We mentioned Perseus's name—this was difficult because I had stopped speaking his name—but I said it out loud that day and declared that I forgave him.

Mrs. Naomi, a mother in the Lord, counseled and prayed for me. She said I should say, "I forgive Perseus," daily. I was prepared to do this consistently. It was a start: my inner healing becoming visible. It might look like a small beginning, but it's a very significant step.

Keep saying it each day until it's true. Whatever your timeline, it's okay.

Forgiveness

I need to forgive
I'm not there.
Jesus is the supreme example of forgiveness,
I must be His disciple.
I'm not there, mercy and truth will guide me.
Your WORD will sustain me.
Your Spirit like a dove will teach me to sing, a new song.
Right now, I need to fly high, above the hawk that is
pursuing my death.
Through the clouds I soar, I see heaven,
Jesus is waving to me to "Come Home!"
I land on His shoulder; I rest close to His head.
Teach me, Lord, show me, explain it more perfectly.

—Bridget Goodwin, 2021

What you can do now: If you're struggling with forgiveness, try writing a letter to your abuser that you'll never send. Express everything you feel—anger, hurt, confusion—without censoring yourself. This release of emotions can be a powerful step toward eventual forgiveness.

Healing with a Personal Cleansing Ritual

The morning of my flight home, it became true.

As I prepared to shower, I reflected on my daily assignment of speaking out loud, *"I forgive..."*

At first, I recoiled, thinking, "Not while I'm naked!"

My body held all the assaults and filth of my abuse. Now I stood naked, and I didn't want to pair his name with my uncovered body. I then had a sense of being challenged; this shouldn't be put off because I remembered how the women of God taught me that weekend: Obey quickly, now!

I said it: "I forgive (name)."

Once again, the name that I hadn't said in months was being spoken. This name that held my pain, the instigator of all my ugly scars that covered my wounded soul. It had to be spoken to identify my trauma. It was quiet, but I said it.

I looked up at the shower head as water poured out, and it dawned on me—God wanted to cleanse me, purify me. I took the soap and washed away all the areas Perseus had contaminated.

"Cleanse every part of me" was my prayer. My tears mixed with the streaming water as I prayed. I washed away the abuse, all the invasions to my physical body. I needed to speak this cleansing as I prayed. It was liberating. You may need to speak your cleansing aloud, too. Name each violation, letting them go as they're washed away, one by one.

Jesus, the healer and restorer, was purifying me. Here in this terrible, run-down, unkempt hotel, a miracle was happening. This is what Jesus does: He comes right to you, where you are in the filth and lowest circumstances, and begins to purge, heal, and restore. You don't need perfection to start your purifying redemption. Jesus's best work happens in the midst of chaos, filth, and turmoil.

I had my hair clipped up, and I heard God say, "Your hair." I started arguing—no, I just washed my hair the other day. He spoke again: "Your hair." My hair was my glory, my covering, as described in the Message Bible:

"Don't you agree there is something naturally powerful in the symbolism—a woman, her beautiful hair reminiscent of angels, praying in adoration; a man, his head bared in reverence, praying in submission?" 1 Corinthians 11:13-16 MSG

My glory, my covering, my hair needed redeeming as well. My abuser had contaminated my covering, this symbol of glory and beauty. He had possessed every aspect of my life physically and spiritually. Jesus wanted me back, to become my glory and cover me, taking back what the enemy stole.

I unclipped my hair and submitted to this voice. I let the water rush down my head, washing it all away. I shampooed and felt the cleansing power.

I needed to cleanse and restore my entire body. Nothing could remain untouched, from the top of my head to the soles of my feet. Water has symbolized cleansing since the Old Testament. In the New Testament, John, Jesus's cousin, immersed this sinless man and baptized Him for our cleansing and for generations to come. I was being made holy in the immersion of this shower water.

He purified me and baptized me completely.

Next, I claimed the blood of Jesus. I prayed, "Let your blood cover *all* of me." Guilt and shame cannot survive where Jesus's blood is applied; they must die. My body and life were bought with the blood of Jesus, and it was time to give it back to Him.

"Or do you not know that your body is a temple of the Holy Spirit within you, whom you have from God? You are not your own, for you were bought with a price. So glorify God in your body." 1 Corinthians 6:19-20 ESV

I felt changed. Speaking it, saying "I forgive (name)" was so critical. And it's vital to obey quickly—because to forgive is divine!

That day in church, I danced, jumped, and twirled like Miriam after the Red Sea parted. She had danced and rejoiced for her freedom, and I was set free, too.

I felt wonderful! I felt renewed! The joy of the Lord was my strength. He is Peace. I'd been made whole. I was safe. I was happy. I rested in His peace because He is Shalom. That day, I was able to forgive my abuser.

I flew home that day with my friend. I looked at her with tears rolling down my face, and told her, "If (Perseus) is in the Kingdom, in Heaven, that's okay—it's between him and God."

That had been my struggle—how could I see him there? Now, it didn't matter. I had let him go. I was truly set free.

What you can do now: Create your own cleansing ritual that speaks to your experience. This might involve water, like a shower or bath, or another symbolic act like writing down what you're releasing and burning the paper. The physical act of cleansing can powerfully reinforce your emotional and spiritual healing.

Heal Yourself Through Forgiving Them All

God didn't stop there. He helped me forgive others involved. As I progressed in my journey of forgiveness, I prayed for others who could have stopped what was happening to me. Some have told me they were sorry, but many have not. Still, I needed to forgive them even if they were never sorry, or never asked for forgiveness. I had to let them go.

When memories and dreams trouble me, I pray for my brain to be healed and changed. I choose the truth, not the lies. I remember being cleansed and forgiven by God. This is truth. Years of abuse can be healed through the restorative power of Jesus. My healing continues. My forgiveness of my abuser was instant. After so much unforgiveness, hate, anger, and rage, *this* was my testimony.

This was monumental! This was a miracle!

Your forgiveness journey may look different from mine, and that's okay—it's your path. It may not be instant; it may be a process over time, or it may seem impossible. One thing is certain: Jesus is your way. Find Him and you'll find your answer, your restoration.

Start Your Healing Journey with Jesus

I've experienced Jesus's rescue and His divine gift of forgiveness. You can experience this, too. If you don't know Jesus, may I help you with a prayer you can pray right now?

"Jesus, I believe that you are my Savior, and only your blood can cleanse me from my sins and shame. I believe you died on the cross for me. I confess that you are Lord. Please come into my heart and forgive me for all my sins. Show me your wonder and let me walk with you. I trust you to save me."

Begin reading His Word—I recommend the book of Psalms and the New Testament. Find a church to support you as you start your new relationship with Jesus.

If you need to renew your relationship with Jesus and recover from your trauma, let me share my prayer with you:

Prayer of Restoration

Lord, I come before you, broken, shattered and lost.
I know you have the power to put me back together again.
Please take all these shattered pieces, and discard the
ones that are not like you.
My heart is broken and my soul feels lost.
Put me back together, and hold me close.
May I feel the safety of Your gentle arms around me.
Let my restored soul and heart reflect your glorious
light and salvation.
You deserve my adoration, my love.
I give you my heart and devotion.
I trust in you, my Savior,
Let the healing begin.
Amen

What you can do now: Find a verse or passage about God's love that resonates with you. Write it on a card and place it somewhere you'll see daily—your bathroom mirror, refrigerator, or as a bookmark. Let this truth gradually reshape how you see yourself and your relationship with the divine.

Why Clergy Abuse Creates Deeper Trauma Than Other Experiences

"Consensual relationships don't result in trauma and lifelong suffering." This is a quote from Christianity Today author, Naghmeh Panahi, and it's something I've found to be true.

But research shows that survivors of adult clergy sexual abuse suffer rates of traumatization that surpass even war veterans. In a study currently being peer-reviewed for publication, professor David Poolerfound 39 percent of adult survivors screened positive for posttraumatic stress disorder, or PTSD. In comparison, under a quarter of US veterans of war had PTSD symptoms. Abuse survivors aren't surprised by this statistic.

This is staggering! Almost half of those who have suffered adult clergy abuse have PTSD. This was me, and it could be you. It's okay if you find yourself in this statistic. You can be helped, and you can survive this. What you're suffering is real—talk to someone who helps you feel safe and validated. Acknowledgment is the first step in starting your healing. Ignoring it won't make it disappear. Your body, mind, and soul deserve self-care and reaching for help from a trusted professional.

Several factors that are unique to clergy abuse led to this higher traumatization rate:

- **Spiritual injury:** The betrayal by someone representing God creates a profound spiritual crisis that compounds psychological trauma (Doehring, 2019)

- **Community loss:** Unlike many other traumas, survivors often lose their entire support system—church community, friendships, and sometimes family relationships—precisely when they most need support (Garland & Argueta, 2010, Pooler & Barros-Lane, 2022)

- **Identity disruption and reconstitution:** For many survivors, religious identity was central to their sense of self, and the abuse forces a profound identity reconstitution (Pargament et al., 2022)

- **Secondary victimization:** Institutional responses that protect perpetrators and silence victims create ongoing traumatization long after the initial abuse ends (McMackin, Keane, Szymanski & Phelps, 2017)

These results highlight the necessity of trauma-informed treatments and contradict the myth that clergy abuse involving adults is less damaging than other types of trauma.

We may not have been on a real battlefield dodging bullets or witnessing death in war, but we've experienced graphic and stunning violations to our bodies and souls. We've fought our own war—it's *real*! And you need and *deserve* help to heal.

I know Jesus can demolish these statistics and restore. I'm living proof—I'm a warrior, a Princess Warrior. You can be a Warrior too.

I offer you the hope and love of Jesus. He loves you and wants to heal you. I told you enough about my trauma to help you without causing more harm. No matter how ugly your story is, He can rewrite your outcome.

You can find your voice, just as I found mine. It's time to find yours.

> **What you can do now:** Consider participating in a trauma-informed support group specifically for religious abuse survivors. While individual therapy is valuable, the shared understanding within a group of people with similar experiences provides unique healing benefits that can accelerate your recovery.

When you step out in courage, you'll be met with liberation. The next poem captures when I first shared my testimony publicly, it was terrifying, I was so afraid. But once I had done it, I was liberated. I was an eagle breaking free of chains.

I Can't Explain This Feeling

Relief, liberation, renewal, how do I explain this feeling?
It is as if I was saved all over again, and I have been cleansed from my past.
I feel different, flying, trying out my new boundaries,
the open sky, not this gilded cage that I have been locked in for the past 40 years.
New sights, a big beautiful horizon is now in view.
I'm not going back, I'm looking ahead!
Watch me fly!!

—Bridget Goodwin, 2021

CHAPTER 13
Where I Am Now & the Beauty in Your Healing Journey

"Healing is not a destination, but a path of countless small victories. I invite you to celebrate every step of your journey." –Bridget

✝

Healing from trauma isn't a neat, linear process with a clear endpoint that points to a sign reading, "You have arrived!" I wish it was this easy.

Everyone's healing journey is vastly different, but they can be strangely similar, too. You *will* get better, you'll be happy again, you'll find that glimmer of hope. Even as I write this, I'm still healing.

Sometimes, beautiful sunshine and hope fill my days, while other days, shadows sneak up and try to pull me into darkness again—but I know how to process these shadows, my fears, and triggers now. I corral them like wild horses and tame them with truth! I'm no longer living in trauma.

I'm free! I'm safe! You can be, too.

I've learned that this is normal, and I want you to know you mustn't put a time limit on your healing. Even after my breakthrough just a few years ago, I'm continuing to heal. Every year that passes is a celebration. Whatever your pace of healing, remember: it isn't failure—it's all part of your journey.

I wish I could say that I'm completely healed when people ask how I am. Don't be upset or embarrassed if you still have more days with triggers than you do days with glimmers. When people ask how I am, I tell them I'm taking it one day at a time, and my good days now outnumber my bad ones.

So, it's safe to say that you're still healing, too.

We must embrace the truth that different aspects of our lives heal at different rates. I still struggle with trust—this part of my trauma is slower to heal. I'm reaching for joy more as I let go of dread. I'm learning to love myself, forgive myself, and thrive when I anchor my thoughts in God's Word and promises. All your broken pieces that were scattered are being put back together in all their complexity to show just how wonderful you are.

Let the process of being put back together happen.

Stop looking for that sign at the end of the road that says, "you have arrived, you are fully healed."

Instead, grab your survival kit and let the tools inside help you navigate your journey—because it *is* a journey. When you are triggered, remind yourself you're not there anymore. When pain sneaks up on you, let your tears cleanse your heart, and hold on to the truth that you're making progress. I've shared my tools of survival which I dearly hope guide you through your journey, and you're discovering your own tools, too.

You're healing. Your pain and triggers will happen, but you'll get past them. Be kind to yourself.

You're strong; you'll thrive, not just survive. I'm right here with you.

What you can do now: Create a "healing timeline" journal where you document small victories, no matter how seemingly insignificant. Each week, review your entries to visually see your progress. This concrete evidence of growth will sustain you during difficult days and remind you that healing is happening, even when it feels slow.

I'm So Broken

Every scattered piece I see is marked with what I have lost.
I long to be put back together, to be whole.
At times I feel complete, joyful, and hopeful.
Then a trigger happens and I'm reminded I'm still
very broken.
I look at my life and the pieces that are scattered, are
fewer
So, I am healing
I just want back what I lost
Time
Youth
Wonder
So many things
I just want what I never had
Anticipation of good things
At times I want to just give up
Maybe I will not be able to be put back together
Maybe I'm too broken
But my heart says wait.
I can't focus on the sharp edges of each broken piece
I must run my hands over the pieces that have been
put together
It is smooth to touch, no rough edges
Each piece oddly shaped are put together as if it were
a puzzle
Each seam sparkles with a glimmer of golden love
that holds each piece together.
It is beautifully broken and whole.
I must let the Master put me back together.
The wait is hard, but He is the mender of all that is
broken.

—Bridget Goodwin, 2025

This poem is here to show you that you may have been broken, but now you can be whole and beautiful. It takes time. I wrote this as I was writing my book and living the memories again. Now I just look for the glimmer of the seam of golden love that is putting me back together. I'm learning to be joyful!

Transform Your Triggers into Stepping Stones

I can recognize my triggers now, and before they devour me, I can reprogram my mind with factual truths. My body may remember the spark of the trigger—a smell, a song, a picture, even a dream, but I can calm myself down, knowing I'm no longer threatened. I can fight this and not go into flight mode.

I tell myself, "This is not happening *now*."

I say to this gut-wrenching feeling, "This isn't present in my life anymore."

If I'm listening to a podcast, YouTube, or social media and hear a preacher who sounds cultish, pushing his religion of *dos* and *don'ts* that isn't Jesus, I can turn it off. I can whisper a prayer of thankfulness that I've been delivered and I'm safe in another church. I can feel relieved that my current pastor is a true follower of Jesus who keeps Him at the center of everything.

As you begin to take control of the small things that trigger you, the bigger things will become easier.

Just changing the channel is a small, but very significant, step toward your recovery. What's happening on the screen, or what you may hear in a relationship is real—it happened or is happening to someone—but you can stop it, leave, change the channel, turn off the music. Tell yourself, "This isn't happening to me now, and it never will ever again."

I've created safe spaces for myself. My husband and my boys, my home, my current church, my circle of friends, even my sweet angel, Lady Elle, my golden retriever—these are 'home' to me.

Remove toxic relationships from your life. There's a quote that says, "You will be hated if you can't be manipulated." What a tough truth to hear—but one we survivors must always keep top of mind.

You may not get everything right, but please prioritize *being safe* over being nice.

I'm still learning how to develop deeper friendships. Good friends have been so important on my healing journey. They've surrounded me with love, care, and prayer. I've been able to let them into my heart with trust because I can be authentic with them. I don't need to hide from my past when I'm with staunch friends, but instead I can share the victories I'm experiencing as God puts me back together. I want you to have that, too.

Our communities—our friends, family, and loved ones are vital. In my case, my husband, Jonathan, has been my rock through this journey. He's been kind, gentle, and compassionate. He's been patient with me as I work through giving myself to him, wholly and completely. He's nurturing our intimacy, and with him I feel love like I've never known. It's pure, beautiful, saturating, and precious—it's rapturous!

I'm learning how to trust, and when I'm caught in the snare of mistrust, my husband talks to me and takes the time to explain and reassure me that things are all right; there are no hidden agendas anymore.

When I'm lost, I have to remind myself to focus. You will, too.

I can have an opinion, disagree with someone in authority, and not be terrified.

I don't have to say *I'm sorry* all the time, or ask if I've done something wrong. As my new pastor told me, "Relax, enjoy the grace, Bridget." What beautiful words of healing and support—it can be so easy to get caught up in our healing, or what we may feel is a lack of it, but what will help us most is remembering God's love for us and the grace he offers us.

I still have the occasional nightmare, but even these have changed. Now, I'm more aggressive. I fight; I stand up for myself and I don't let Perseus win anymore. I no longer wake up screaming, and I don't always need to have the light on if I'm alone at night.

These are extraordinary victories for me because I've *survived* my experience. My trauma has become a scar—no longer an open wound.

My husband is encouraging me to move beyond seeing myself as a *victim* and embrace being a *conqueror*. I encourage you to find a new perspective where you can feel empowered, too.

As I've mentioned before, *you* are my ministry—my mission field.

Writing this book has been a tremendous healing channel for me. It has taken longer than I thought it would to get the story down in a way that's healing for both you, my fellow survivor, and me, but what lives here now in these pages is, I hope, medicine for us both.

I don't need to escape from my pain because I'm healing *through* each painful memory. Even today, a memory might explode in my head, but I can address it, forgive—the other person or myself—if needed, and replace that painful memory with new truth.

For example, I remind myself I'm not that person anymore, or trapped in that past circumstance; Jesus has rescued me from the dark cave. I'm not clothed in shame and doom. I don't have to dread the future but instead, I can grab hold of life with joy. I can be excited again, from the smallest thing to the biggest. Memories can become messengers, not nagging voices of torment. I can deal with them. I can choose not to be defined by them anymore.

Whatever I need in that moment, I just grab from the many resources in my toolbox.

My top tools are setting aside time to pray, reading God's Word, journaling, and worshiping with my favorite music. You will find your favorite tools, too.

When I speak to you and other survivors, loved ones of survivors, or host workshops through I Have a Voice Ministries, I'm no longer hiding from my past. I'm using my voice that was once silenced to herald the way to healing—a clear clarion call. A guide, a map, a kit filled with tools to help you discover your own road to healing. I share my champion, my hope, my deliverer: JESUS.

What you can do now: Create your own "safe space" inventory. List the people, places, activities, and practices that bring you genuine peace and safety. Then intentionally schedule more time in these spaces. When triggered, consciously retreat to one of these safe zones until your nervous system calms. This practical routine builds resilience over time.

The Unique Rhythm of Your Healing

Time alone doesn't heal trauma, but healing requires time. This is still confusing to me to this day! At times, I feel whole, knowing I'm moving ahead, then—*bam!*—something sets me back.

So, I take a moment to regroup. Here are some things I may do as I heal in this gentle container of time:

Let the tears of doubt cleanse me; share with a friend and ask for prayer; recall that my recovery time is much shorter now; look for the glimmer of hope; and renounce the triggers. Above all, I remind myself I'm a *victor*, not a victim anymore!

This is why healing happens in spirals rather than a straight line—it's rarely linear. You'll revisit certain wounds, but each time from a different perspective with new resources. You may even come to realize that you're showing signs your wound is developing a scar.

YOU ARE HEALING!

What triggered or overwhelmed you might become manageable today. Your voice, which may seem like a whisper, will feel strong enough to speak. Your prayers will flow freely because you're being released from different mindsets.

Different aspects of trauma heal at different rates. Physical symptoms might resolve quickly with proper support. Trust often requires years of consistent safety to rebuild. Spiritual healing may happen in sudden breakthroughs or gradual reconciliations. Relational patterns might need conscious rebuilding over decades.

Your timeline is yours, no one else's. If you compare, you're only robbing yourself of your healing. Even my healing differs from how yours will flow. Your journey is uniquely yours, influenced by factors beyond your control: the nature of your trauma, your access to resources, your support system, even your neurobiological makeup.

What you can do now: Draw a spiral on paper to represent your healing journey. Mark significant breakthroughs, setbacks, and current challenges along this spiral. This visual reminder shows that revisiting difficult emotions isn't regression—it's encountering familiar territory from a new vantage point with greater resources and strength than before.

Navigate Every Stage of Your Healing Journey

For Those Just Beginning

If you're just starting your healing journey, I want you to know this: the fact that you've opened this book is already an act of immense courage. The first steps are often the hardest, when the pain feels most acute and the path forward least clear.

Start with safety. Find one person you can trust—a therapist, a support group leader, a trauma-informed spiritual director. Safety isn't just physical; it's emotional and spiritual, too. You deserve spaces where your experience is believed, where your boundaries are respected, where your pace is honored.

Expect resistance from those who benefited from your silence. Not everyone will celebrate your healing, especially if it involves speaking truths others have worked to keep hidden. This doesn't mean you're wrong—often it confirms you're finally getting it right.

Be patient with your body. Trauma lives in our tissues, our nervous systems, our unconscious responses. Your body protected you during trauma in the only way it knew how. Now, it needs gentle retraining to recognize safety. Movement and breathwork can help your body catch up to what your mind is learning.

For Those in the Middle

The middle of the healing journey can feel like a wilderness—you've left the familiar shores of silence but haven't yet reached the promised land of wholeness. This liminal space is sacred, though it rarely feels that way. Take comfort; you've started your transition to healing!

When progress seems slow, look backward periodically to see how far you've come. The panic attacks that once came daily might now come only monthly. The shame that once colored every thought might now just tint some moments. These subtle shifts matter profoundly.

Find companions for this stretch of the journey. Whether through formal support groups, trusted friends who understand trauma, or professional guides, connection combats the isolation trauma creates. Your brain literally heals differently in safe relationships than it does in isolation.

Notice not just what still hurts, but what has begun to feel pleasurable again. Can you enjoy music? Taste food fully? Feel the warmth of sunlight? The return of sensory pleasure often precedes intellectual understanding of healing.

For Those Who Feel Healed

If you've reached a place of substantial healing, celebrate this miracle while staying gentle with yourself during inevitable setbacks. Healing is rarely a one-and-done process, but rather a spiral of growth that occasionally revisits old territory.

Maintain boundaries even when you feel strong. Healing doesn't mean you need to test yourself by engaging with toxic people or situations. Your well-being matters too much to sacrifice for someone else's comfort or convenience.

Consider how your healing might become hope for others. This doesn't mean you must become a public advocate; sharing your wisdom with even one other survivor creates ripples of healing. If you feel led to write or form a circle of healing for others like you, do it with love, mercy, and care. Your hard-won insights are medicine for a wounded world.

Remember that continued healing isn't always a forward motion. If new dimensions of your trauma surface years later, this isn't failure, but your life, body, and spirit continuing a movement toward wholeness.

The deeper layers often emerge only when you're strong enough to face them.

Dr. B told me at my last session with him that if I needed to return to therapy after he released me, that was okay. As a therapist, he knew that old wounds sometimes resurface. We have resources—you don't need to do it alone even if you think you're strong enough. In those moments of vulnerability, seek a power source of strength.

I love this quote from a wonderful friend, and I think of it frequently: "Setbacks are future setups."

What you can do now: Identify where you are on your healing journey—beginning, middle, or feeling substantially healed—and create a self-care plan specifically for your current phase. Early healing requires basic safety and validation, the middle journey needs companionship and visible progress markers, while later stages benefit from boundary maintenance and finding meaning in your experience.

Create Your Ripples of Healing

Your healing matters beyond your individual life. When you heal, you create possibility for others. I remember a good friend calling me out of the blue and offering loving words of comfort. She told me my life was going to cause a ripple effect to help others—the ripples would start small but would expand and grow.

Her beautiful words truly sat with me. I didn't know that the year following this phone call would be the year I dropped my small pebble into a once-silent river, and I would use my voice to help me and others. I've witnessed this ripple effect through my ministry—one person's brave disclosure creates space for another's, then another's, until an entire community transforms.

Sometimes, we survivors need to feel as if our healing helps others before we can truly dig into the work. Your children and grandchildren benefit from your healing work, too. Research confirms that trauma can be passed on generationally, through epigenetics—but so can resilience. Every step you take toward wholeness reshapes the future for those who follow you. Through awareness and bravery, trauma can stop right here—with you!

Communities heal when individuals heal.

The church has been both a source of deep wounds, and an instrument of recovery. As more survivors find their voices, religious communities face necessary reckonings that, while painful, create a possibility for authentic spiritual community built on truth rather than silence.

Understand the Science Behind Your Healing Journey

Research confirms that trauma recovery follows a nonlinear trajectory. Longitudinal studies of trauma survivors show that healing typically involves periods of significant progress followed by plateaus or temporary setbacks before further growth occurs (Calhoun & Tedeschi, 2014).

Brain imaging studies reveal why healing continues throughout life. Traumatic experiences physically alter brain structures and neural pathways. Recovery involves the growth of new neural connections that integrate traumatic memories into a coherent narrative, a process that continues over decades (van der Kolk, 2014).

The concept of Post-Traumatic Growth helps explain positive transformations years after trauma. Research by Tedeschi and Calhoun identifies five domains where survivors often experience growth: greater appreciation for life, more meaningful relationships, increased sense of personal strength, recognition of new possibilities, and spiritual development.

And studies of clergy abuse survivors specifically show that healing often involves a multi-dimensional process that includes: reclamation of spiritual identity separate from institutional religion, development of voice and agency after silencing, integration of traumatic experiences into a coherent narrative, establishment of boundaries and safety practices, and reconnection with embodiment after dissociative responses.

You can see how these facets of healing intertwine, and through my story, you can see how each one was critical for my own healing. Seeing one person heal is like hearing about the first man to break a four-minute mile. No one thought it could be done, but as soon as a man named Roger Bannister ran a mile in under four minutes, back in 1954, it only took one more month for another person to beat a four-minute mile, too. We are inspired by others' achievements and it proves to us it can be done.

And research on resilience shows that continued healing throughout life is not only common, but *expected*. Dr. Ann Masten calls it 'ordinary magic'—a natural skill we develop throughout our life to adapt in situations of hardship (Masten, 2014).

What you can do now: Learn about one aspect of trauma science that resonates with your experience—perhaps neuroplasticity, intergenerational trauma, or post-traumatic growth. Understanding the biological and psychological processes of trauma recovery normalizes your experience and provides hope that your brain and body are designed to heal, even from severe trauma.

Lessons I've Learned on My Healing Journey

My journey to forgiveness taught me that true healing happens when we release others for our *own* freedom, not theirs.

I discovered forgiveness isn't a one-time event but a process that primarily benefits me by cutting the invisible tether binding me to my abuser. Most importantly, I learned that forgiveness doesn't require reconciliation, an apology, or relinquishing justice—it's about freeing my heart from the weight of hatred that was never mine to carry. Even now, I sometimes need to reaffirm my forgiveness when triggers resurface.

This isn't failure; it's part of the journey.

What surprised me most was how physical my healing needed to be. Trauma lives in the body, not just the mind, which is why the shower cleansing ritual became so powerful for me. The water, my spoken words, and the intentional cleansing of my body—especially my hair—created a sacred space where Jesus met me in my vulnerability. I've found that healing integrates mind, body, and spirit, often requiring us to find our own unique healing symbols and practices. For me, this came through community support—trusted guides who appeared when I was ready, witnessing my journey and walking alongside me as I found my voice. Your healing path may look different, but you won't find it alone.

Finding my voice became the ultimate expression of my power. Each time I share my story, I reclaim another stolen piece of myself. What began as a whisper has grown stronger with each telling, transforming my wounds into words that can protect others. After four decades of silence, my voice now brings life and hope to those in darkness.

Your voice—once found—will do the same.

It becomes a sacred instrument of change, turning your past suffering into purpose. This is how we become warriors, fighting not with weapons of hatred but with a truth that sets others free.

Continue Your Healing Journey with Hope

The healing journey has no fixed endpoint this side of heaven, and that's not bad news—it's liberation from the pressure of *arriving*. Instead, we grow continually more awake, more compassionate, more whole. Some days I still struggle, and some days I soar—but every day, I'm healing.

If I could leave you with one truth, it would be this: You aren't broken beyond repair. No matter how severe your trauma, how long you've carried it, or how many setbacks you've experienced, healing is possible. Not always perfect healing, not always complete erasure of pain, but genuine transformation that allows you to live fully and joyfully despite what happened to you.

Your voice matters—whether you speak to one trusted friend or to thousands through public advocacy. Your healing matters—not just for you but for everyone your life touches.

Your journey matters—with all its unique twists and turns, setbacks and breakthroughs.

Memories still come up unexpectedly for me sometimes. I still encounter triggers that momentarily transport me back. But I now have resources, fellowship, and a strong faith to help. Real healing means having resources to face things gracefully, not wholly symptom-free living.

Wherever you are in your journey, whether taking your first tentative steps toward healing or walking steadily on a well-worn path, know this: you aren't alone. Your story matters. Your healing is possible. And your voice, once found, has a power beyond measure.

My Final Words to You

Let me share with you again my scripture—that I held onto and quoted during my greatest anxiety attacks—from David the Psalmist in Psalms 16:8:

"I have set the Lord always before me; because he is at my right hand, I shall not be shaken..."

I'm happy to say that now I'm embracing the rest of this passage with joy, holding Jesus' hand still but not crushing it for dear life because of fear. I'm enjoying the journey with Him as I dwell in His safety:

"Therefore my heart is glad, and my whole being rejoices; my flesh also dwells secure."

You will rejoice again.

Just keep walking, one step at a time.

Rest along the way.

Keep healing.

Keep speaking.

Take my hand, I'm walking right with you.

You are not alone.

Epilogue
1 Corinthians 13

The words of 1 Corinthians 13 have echoed through countless weddings, decorated inspirational posters, and resonated in sermons throughout Christian history. Yet for those who've experienced abuse at the hands of religious leaders who twisted these very scriptures, reclaiming these sacred words becomes an essential part of the healing journey.

As I traveled toward wholeness, I needed to redefine love on my own terms—not according to the false definitions given by my abuser, but according to divine truth that truly sets captives free. This rewriting represents my reclamation of scripture that was once weaponized against me, now transformed into a powerful declaration of liberation.

I offer these words as both my testimony and an invitation for you to reclaim whatever sacred texts or beliefs have been distorted in your experience. True love—whether human or divine—never exploits, never controls, never destroys. It always protects, always trusts, always hopes, always perseveres.

This is my anthem. This is my story of love. I want to herald it, unmuted, from the highest mountaintop to the deepest valley, from the darkest cave to the open plains, from the tumultuous seas to the calmest lake. It works! If you have love, you have Jesus, and that is everything.

Consider a text, scripture, song, or saying that was used to harm you or keep you silent. Write your own reclaimed version that speaks truth and liberation instead. This act of rewriting transforms what was once weaponized against you into a source of strength and healing. Keep this new version where you can see it daily as a reminder of your power to define truth for yourself.

And if it resonates with you, I invite you to take into your heart my adapted version of 1 Corinthians 13.

I Corinthians 13 (Bridget's Version)

I speak from the heart of love, from the recovery
side of abuse. Love has threads that make the heartbeat.
My heart has been transformed by the price of
ultimate love, the blood of my Savior Jesus as He
died for me on the cross at Calvary.
I am rich in His love.
My heart beats with the threads of His love,
redemption, hope, restoration, release, and rhapsody!
Abuse was not love....this IS love.
I'm not caged, silenced, but I'm free, ready to sing of
LOVE.
Love doesn't target to hurt or harm but is patient not
making demands from your character flaws, but
takes the time to walk beside you allowing your
tender years of innocence to be protected.
Love is not cruel with shame creating fear and
seclusion, but is kind, and allows friendship of
family, and others.
Love is not excessive with jealousy, putting you down
for your vibrant personality, allowing you to not
smile, laugh and speak with others, but directs you to
others that need your positive voice and smile,
secure and not threatened by your love to others.
Love doesn't break the rules of integrity to promote
its hidden agenda, but is modest, careful to not break
the heart of the broken, it follows the rule that love
wins, and hate destroys.
Love does not ridicule nor humiliates demanding its
needs with aggressive rudeness, but is accepting that
your welfare, safety and position is to be respected
and honored.
Love doesn't seek its agenda on how you can be
enslaved, meeting their endless desires one by one,
but makes you feel significant, worthy, your needs
being put first.
Love is not aggressive, provoked in brutality through

a mask of gentleness, but is sensitive, real, genuine, moved with peaceful empathy, patient.

Love is not hateful, full of resentment, keeping score of every violation they have imagined and provoked from you, but it is gracious, extending unmeasured grace, never making you error in violation to protect yourself.

Love doesn't keep score, sarcastically recalling every error, skeptical of your every move, too selfish to celebrate your life, but love gives you a party, a reason to live with joy, ecstatic to celebrate your accomplishments, not failures.

Love does not calculate the passing of time to ensnare you, prowling in the shadows, looking for a way to capture you unaware, off guard, but love sees your innocence and vulnerability and protects you, endures the time it takes for you to grow in wisdom that only time will teach you.

Love does not promote a false identity in you. This gives them pleasure, overtaking your purpose, clouding your vision, truth becomes distorted, but love seeks the destiny of truth, clarity of your purpose, the vision of a destiny that is the beauty of you, your hopes, your dreams.

Love does not control your day, your week, or your years with the weapons of fear, isolation and control, but love lets you fly, soaring with great confidence knowing you will never be caged, you are free to love and have joy.

Love does not drown you with its lust of perverted desires that can't be satisfied, love never violates you with harm and rejection. Love seeks to restore you and to protect you, it will never rob you! This love can never be measured, it is endless.

Love doesn't demand devotion with "their" religious rituals by using the Sacred Tools of God, manipulating God's Divine Word for their perverted agenda, but love seeks for the intimate relationship of Jesus, rejecting all works of the flesh, and ritual devotions. It is a marriage of love, walking daily with Jesus, speaking the WORD, living in total devotion because one is cherished and valued.

Love will never sacrifice the one that is vulnerable, to promote itself. Love will sacrifice itself to preserve the weak, to heal the sick, to set the prisoner free.

Love is not a parasite, stalking to kill and destroy, gleaning the benefits until they are no longer useful, casting aside ready to conquer the next victim. Abuse comes in many forms, sexual, physical, mental, and sadly even in houses of religion.

Love will seek you, to save you.

Love will pursue you, to help you.

Love will protect you to keep you from harm.

Love will surround you to make you feel safe.

Love will praise you, so you feel accepted.

Love will forgive you to shew you mercy.

Love speaks truth so you will not be deceived.

Love never fails, it is ageless.

Love is the blood of the Lamb.

Love is your Heavenly Father, that gave His only Son, Jesus.

May your heart throb with every thread of love that is from above, all together lovely and divine, for it lives within you, a treasured gift from God, Jesus His Son!

—Bridget

From reclaiming scripture to reclaiming joy—that's the journey. After years of being told I had no voice, no right to celebrate, no permission to simply be free, I discovered that freedom itself is a form of worship. The little California girl who once rode her bike into the sunset? She's dancing now. And she's reaching back for you, because no one should stay in darkness when the light is here.

This is my invitation.

This is my hand extended.

I Dance, We Dance

I dance, I jump, I turn, why? Because I have been set free.
The chains that held me, crippled me and paralyzed
me have been unlocked, broken and demolished.
Jesus had the key, He released me!
The TRUTH has set me free.
Tears of joy shimmer on my vibrant face!
I reach for your hand, let's dance, let's leap, we are free!
We laugh, we giggle, we dance in His glorious light,
no more darkness, no more hiding, no more feeling
trapped!
I search for you, I can hear your chains rattle, let me
introduce you to my Deliverer, JESUS.
I see your face, tears of sadness, eyes full of fear, you
are shaking in desperation.
His loving arms reach to you, He unlocks every
chain, He takes time to demolish each one.
He opens His arms to you; He gives you shelter in
His warm embrace.
He calms your disturbed heart and soul.
Healing oil, He puts on every wound left from the chains.
He sings to you, as He gently calls your name.
He restores your strength, He is HOPE.
You will dance again, you will smile, you will cry, but
this time, tears of joy.
Grab my hand, we are safe, free to dance in His
glorious light, no longer victims, but victors!

—Bridget Goodwin, 2022

Your Homecoming

The California girl on the blue Schwinn bike never really disappeared. She waited, patient and persistent, through decades of darkness. She waited through the cage, through the silence, through the years when I couldn't remember who

I was before the abuse began. She waited because she knew something I had forgotten: freedom was always my birthright.

I wrote this book for her—for that innocent child whose bike was left behind, whose voice was stolen, whose joy was crushed under the weight of religious manipulation and abuse. I wrote it to tell her she was never forgotten, never truly lost, never beyond redemption.

But I also wrote this book for you.

If you're reading these words and you see yourself in my story—if you recognize the patterns, feel the familiar weight of chains, hear the echo of your own silenced voice—please know this: your California girl is waiting too. That person you were before the abuse, before the control, before you learned to make yourself small and quiet and compliant? That person is still inside you. Waiting. Hoping. Ready to ride free again.

The journey to wholeness isn't easy. There were days I wanted to give up, moments when the darkness felt too thick, times when I couldn't remember what freedom even felt like. But Jesus never let go. He held the key to every chain. He sang over me in the silence. He reminded me, again and again, that I was His daughter—beloved, treasured, worth fighting for.

You are worth fighting for too.

My healing workshops exist because I know what it's like to feel utterly alone in this journey. I know the shame, the confusion, the fear of speaking your truth. I know how it feels when people don't believe you, when churches protect predators instead of survivors, when the very scriptures you loved are twisted into weapons against you. I've walked that road, and I'm walking it still—because healing isn't a destination, it's a daily choice to keep moving toward the light.

But here's what I've learned: you don't have to walk it alone.

The chains can break. The voice can return. The joy—that deep, unshakeable joy that comes from knowing you are loved by the Creator of the universe—can be yours again. Not someday. Not when you've "done enough healing" or "gotten over it." Now. Today. This moment.

I'm on the other side now, wind in my hair, pedaling into the sunset of a life I never dared to imagine. I'm dancing in the freedom I thought was lost forever. I'm singing songs that were silenced for too long. I'm becoming, finally, the woman God always intended me to be.

And I'm reaching back for you.

Take my hand. Let's dance. Let's leap. Let's ride our bikes into the sunset together—free, healed, whole, and victoriously, beautifully alive.

The California girl inside you is ready.

Let's go home.

Walking Alongside Her: A Husband's Perspective

Walking this journey with Bridget has been a rollercoaster ride, to say the least. One of the first things I want to tell you is this: it's totally worth it in the end. While the lows can be devastating and the highs exhilarating—your emotions stretched from one extreme to the other—by God's grace and by walking through the struggle, you do end up in a much better place.

Heroes are born out of adversity—no fight, no hero. Think of any great story—whether comedy, adventure, or romance—they all follow a similar formula: first comes the problem, then the introduction of the character(s) who will become heroes, next the grueling process of overcoming, and finally, the celebration.

As you read Bridget's story, you'll see why she is my hero. The problem was massive. The character (Bridget) is deeply human. The process was unclear and painful. But the celebration—oh, it's out of this world.

You may think you know the solution: forgiveness. And yes, to forgive is divine. But that one word carries more weight than we often realize. The entire plan of salvation is built on forgiveness. Yet it's been said that if anything ever taxed God, it was how to forgive humanity. Four thousand years after Adam fell, Jesus stepped onto the scene to purchase our forgiveness. The timing had to be right, the character flawless, the process perfect, the Spirit divine—and the love... limitless.

We're still trying to comprehend what forgiveness truly cost. Entire libraries have been filled, podcasts recorded, movies made, and countless sermons preached about that singular act on the cross. So, when someone casually says, "Just forgive them," it reveals a complete lack of understanding of what forgiveness truly entails.

Bridget is completely open and honest in sharing her journey. There is no doubt in my mind that writing this book is the right thing to do, for you see, this is God's story and it is all about Him and His amazing grace made manifest in and through forgiveness. I've told Bridget many times that she has taught me more about God through this experience than I ever expected. If God could save her through all of this—and He did an absolutely incredible job—then He can do the same for you.

I'm reminded of the Apostle Paul's words in Romans 15:4:

"Whatever was written in former times was written for our instruction, that through endurance and the encouragement of the Scriptures we might have hope." Your story may be different. Your suffering may be deeper. The characters in your story may still be with you. But no matter your situation, I know Bridget's story will become a source of comfort and hope for you. As you walk patiently, take heart: the celebration is coming.

Bridget asked me to write something from the perspective of the one walking beside her through this hardship. I hesitated. This story isn't about me—and I never wanted my beautiful wife to feel she brought me pain. But for your benefit—the one walking with someone through their suffering—I'll share some things that helped me and may help you, too.

1. Recognize the True Source of Your Pain

It wasn't my wife who brought sorrow into my life. She is the victim. The perpetrator—and those who failed to protect her—bear that responsibility. Those who ignored red flags, those who blindly believed one man's words, and those who remained silent—all of them share in the harm. Some even found out and, instead of apologizing, washed their hands of it like Pilate. That spirit is anti-Gospel. Jesus bore the sins of others. Nehemiah and Daniel included themselves in the sins of their fathers. But today, too many choose to hide or minimize wrongdoing. Run from people who refuse to acknowledge harm—they cannot help you heal.

2. Surround Yourself with People Who Bring Light

Whether you're the victim or walking beside one, you need a support system. Some may be long-distance encouragers, but you need a few close ones—people who can meet you for coffee, pray with you, and truly listen. Choose wisely. Some will misuse your vulnerability. Be careful who you let in.

3. Prepare for Moments of Darkness—But Don't Live There

When Bridget told me the full truth, I was shattered. I couldn't eat for days. I didn't want to speak. I didn't even want to exist. My world exploded. Bridget feared our marriage might not survive—and honestly, I wasn't sure either. But God was merciful. I tried talking to someone I trusted, but their advice was the worst I could have received. They told me, "Separate the man from the message." But you can't do that with Jesus. You can't claim His message and ignore His character. The same principle applies. Truth without integrity isn't truth at all.

4. Find a Skilled Guide for the Journey

Bridget and I were living in London at the time. We were pastoring a church affiliated with the very group led by her abuser. That church had no intention of cutting ties. I didn't believe God wanted us to leave. But then, someone I didn't even know gave me a warning:

"If you don't leave, you'll lose your marriage, your church, and eventually your life."

Within six months, Bridget nearly left. Six months later, I had a heart attack. I remember lying in that hospital bed and hearing a quiet voice ask, "Will you believe Me now?" Four months after that, we moved back to the U.S.

I struggled to find work. My pastoral experience wasn't translating into jobs. Financially, we were drowning. I felt like less of a man every day. Eventually, my family booked me a session with a Christian psychologist—someone with a military background, which felt strangely perfect. That therapist helped me uncover lies I believed about God and life. Most importantly, he helped me process my wife's abuse. It was through him that Bridget began her own path to healing.

Therapy changed our lives. Please—find a good one.

5. Create a Haven of Safety and Understanding

Safety meant Bridget could tell me anything she felt I needed to know—without fear of judgment. Not all the painful details, but the things relevant to healing. She needed to know I wasn't angry at her. That my words and actions were rooted in love.

Loneliness is a cruel companion for victims. Many were abused in isolation and told never to speak. Being that one safe, listening person helped Bridget begin to speak to her therapist. That gave her the courage to share with others. Telling a victim to "just be quiet" is one of the worst things you can do.

6. Walk with Patience

This journey of healing and forgiveness is long. Yes, God can heal instantly—but often, the road winds through valleys and there are setbacks. Sometimes you'll move forward, sometimes you'll need to step back. Just remember: God is with you every step of the way.

To you walking through your own story—or walking beside someone else—my prayer is this: may you become another hero. Not because you're perfect, but because you chose to stay, to love, to heal, and to hope.

If you're supporting someone through trauma, create a self-care routine that helps you process your own emotions. This might include talking with a trusted friend, journaling, physical activity, or therapy. Supporting others through trauma can create secondary trauma in caregivers, and your own emotional health is crucial for providing continued support to your loved one.

— Jonathan Goodwin

ACKNOWLEDGEMENTS

Jesus, and Father God, without you this would not have been possible. Thank you for the gift of redemption. You are my everything, my all in all.

Johnny, you have carried my baggage. I hope you feel that the load is a bit lighter. I love you, always and forever.

Sam and Josiah, you have loved, supported me, and held my hand. I'm so proud of you both.

Anthony and Judy, you believed me and gave me my first opportunity to share my testimony.

Rob and Julie, you gave me a safe environment to share for the first time in your church. Of course, I will never forget you running to my side, Julie, when I needed support.

Sue, you stayed up with me the night before I shared my testimony and listened, offering sound wisdom because I was struggling. You are always a tower of strength to me.

Lil' Nina (Christina), you have been at my side, always cheering me on.

All my friends that have listened, walked with me, cried with me, wiped my tears, held me, prayed with me and for me, dropped everything and drove across the state to comfort me. I could not have made it this far without you.

Holly, for helping me put it all on paper.

Pastor Stuart, you have been a shepherd after God's own heart. Thanks for giving me a place to rest.

APPENDIX
& Resources

Recommended Resources for Help

Books

- **The Body Keeps the Score: Brain, Mind, and Body in the Healing of Trauma** by Bessel A. van der Kolk, M.D.
- **The Devil Inside** by Jimmy Hinton
- **Healing Every Day – A 90-Day Devotional Journey** by Mary DeMuth
- **Into the Light** by Mary DeMuth

Websites

- childhelp.org
- choosingtherapy.com
- christianpsychological.org
- clergysexualmisconduct.com
- crisistextline.org
- dianelangberg.com
- healthline.com
- ncadv.org
- netgrace.org
- ptsd.uk
- rainn.org
- restoredvoicescollective.com
- safeharborim.com
- thehopeofsurvivors.com
- thehotline.org
- victimconnect.org
- 988lifeline.org

Crisis Hotlines

- Childhelp National Child Abuse Hotline: 1-800-422-4453
- National Domestic Violence Hotline: 1-800-799-Safe (7233)
- National Sexual Assault Hotline: 1-800-656-HOPE (4673)
- VictimConnect Resource Center: 1-855-4-victim (855-484-2846)
- For Immediate Danger: Always call 911 or your local emergency number

Professional Help Guidance

Searching for Trauma Informed Therapists

- psychologytoday.com/us/therapists
- emdr International Association – emdria.org
- the national child traumatic stress network – nctsn.org

I Have a Voice Ministry – for workshops, retreats, and healing circles

- Website: ihaveavoice.love
- Bridget's mission: "giving a voice to those who have been silenced through sexual abuse. your story matters. your voice deserves to be heard."
- Safe spaces to share, heal and find community
- licensed therapists and counselors available

Warning Signs of Spiritual Abuse

Red Flags: How to Spot Spiritual Manipulation

These patterns of manipulation appeared early in my story and often exist in religious environments where abuse occurs:

1. Charismatic authority figures:

- Leaders who command unusual levels of respect or admiration
- Authority figures who generate intense emotional responses
- People placed on a pedestal

2. Inappropriate attention toward children:

- Singling out specific children for special attention
- Expressing unusual interest in taking a child away from parents
- Requesting photos or mementos of specific children

3. Boundary violations:

- Attempting to visit a family's home despite objections
- Persistent contact through calls after initial advances are rebuffed
- Undermining existing relationships (like Perseus did with Pastor Parson)

4. Division and isolation:

- Creating divisions within communities
- Forcing people to choose sides

- Separating families from supportive communities

5. Urgency and pressure:

- Rapid, pressured decision-making about major life changes
- Sudden relocations
- Leaving possessions behind
- Feeling compelled to decide quickly to please an authority figure

Recognizing Common Patterns of Clergy Misconduct

Though every case of clergy sexual misconduct is distinct, research reveals shared patterns that survivors commonly experience. These patterns typically begin with an imbalance of power between the spiritual leader and those under their care.

The cycle often unfolds in predictable stages: Survivors frequently enter these situations already vulnerable—seeking spiritual guidance, dealing with past trauma, or facing financial dependence through ministry employment. Their trust in leadership and dedication to faith can increase susceptibility.

Perpetrators systematically groom their targets by building trust, meeting emotional needs, creating isolation, and establishing dependency. They often groom entire communities simultaneously to deflect accountability. Boundary violations escalate gradually from inappropriate conversations to physical contact.

Once abuse begins, victims experience profound confusion and guilt that silences them. Perpetrators employ gaslighting to distort victims' reality and project blame, convincing targets they caused or consented to the behavior. Scripture may be twisted to justify actions. Control intensifies through manipulation, fear, and coercion, sometimes escalating to violence. Victims may develop trauma bonding that mimics affection. The resulting psychological impact manifests as deteriorating mental and physical health, including brain fog, anxiety, appetite changes, self-harm, and suicidal ideation—often invisible to outsiders.

Disclosure frequently brings additional trauma. Survivors commonly face victim-blaming while their abuse is mislabeled as an "affair" or consensual relationship. They may be branded with terms like "Jezebel spirit" or pressured to apologize.

Churches typically protect perpetrators, using euphemisms like "moral failure" instead of acknowledging abuse. Leaders often face minimal consequences and may return to ministry positions. Survivors can develop PTSD from both the original abuse and the institutional response. However, healing remains possible through professional trauma therapy and survivor support networks.

For more detailed information on clergy sexual misconduct patterns, visit clergysexualmisconduct.com.

The Grooming Process in Clergy Abuse

Research into clergy abuse has identified consistent patterns in how predatory clergy groom their victims. A comprehensive study by Garland & Argueta (2014) identified distinct stages in the grooming process:

- **Special Attention:** Predators identify vulnerable individuals and provide extraordinary attention, creating a sense of being "chosen"
- **Relationship Building:** The perpetrator establishes trust through mentoring, counseling, or special roles
- **Boundary Violations:** Small boundary crossings that gradually increase in severity, often framed as "ministry" or "spiritual guidance"
- **Secret Keeping:** Creating situations of secrecy and isolation, often using spiritual language about "sacred confidentiality"
- **Spiritual Manipulation:** Using theological concepts to justify inappropriate behavior and silence victims

Difficulties after Disclosure

- Victim is often retraumatized when speaking out through victim-blaming

- Abuse is frequently mislabeled as an "affair" or consensual relationship
- Victim may be wrongly labeled with terms like "spirit of Jezebel"
- Victim may be improperly counseled to apologize or take responsibility
- Victim may accept blame before understanding the abuse
- Victim may receive harmful or inadequate counseling
- Church often protects the leader, who may face minimal consequences
- Churches often use euphemisms like "moral failure" rather than addressing the abuse
- Leader may later return to ministry where abuse can continue
- Survivor's marriage may experience strain
- Survivor can develop PTSD from both abuse and subsequent treatment
- Survivors can find healing through professional therapy and support groups.

Protect Your Healing by Recognizing These Warning Signs

Here are some patterns that can disrupt the healing process. Be aware of these warning signs so that you can keep your healing journey moving forward.

Watch for Timeline Pressure

- Expectations of being completely healed by a certain point
- Measuring your progress against others' timelines
- Being told, "It's been long enough now"
- Shame about continuing to struggle years later
- Pressure to move on or let it go
- Expectations that healing should be linear or predictable

Avoid Spiritual Bypassing

- Using spirituality to avoid dealing with emotional wounds
- Premature forgiveness before processing anger and grief
- Rushing to positive thinking without acknowledging pain
- Focusing only on heavenly redemption while ignoring earthly justice
- Shame about normal trauma responses (nightmares, triggers, etc.)
- Being told your continued suffering shows a lack of faith

Recognize When Others Minimize Your Needs

- Believing you shouldn't need support anymore
- Shame about seeking continued therapy or counseling
- Hiding ongoing struggles to appear healed
- Pushing yourself into triggering situations to prove you're over it
- Ignoring body signals that suggest continuing trauma responses
- Dismissing the need for ongoing self-care practices

Don't Isolate Yourself

- Withdrawing from support systems as symptoms improve
- Believing you should handle remaining challenges alone
- Hesitation to share continuing struggles for fear of judgment
- Feeling you've burdened others enough already
- Thinking no one will understand the subtle nature of later-stage healing
- Shame about reaching out when things get difficult again

Reject False Teaching

- "Real healing means never having another symptom."
- "If you still struggle, you haven't truly forgiven."
- "Complete healing happens in this lifetime."
- "Strong Christians shouldn't need ongoing support."

- "Your healing should follow the same pattern as theirs."
- "Time heals all wounds without additional intervention."

Scripture References

Bibles

- The Message Bible – Especially the Book of Psalms
- The Holy Bible – English Standard Version, NIV & KJV

Biblical Truths for Healing

God's Love:

- Sets free (Galatians 5:1)
- Invites and pursues gently (Matthew 11:28)
- Never forces or manipulates (Revelation 3:20)
- Brings peace, not fear (I John 4:18)
- Cast Out shame (Romans 8:1)
- Encourages discernment (1John 4:1)

Bible Verses on God's Love vs. Control

God's Nature is Love – Foundational Verses about Who God is

- 1 John 4:8 (ESV) "Anyone who does not love does not know God, because God is love."
- Romans 5:8 (ESV) " But God shows his love for us in that while we were still sinners, Christ died for us."
- Zephaniah 3:17 (ESV) "The Lord your God is in your midst, a might one who will save; he will rejoice over you with gladness; he will quiet you by his love; he will exult over you with loud singing."

God Gives Us the Freedom to Choose

- Galatians 5:1 (ESV) "For freedom Christ has set us free; stand firm therefore, and do not submit again to a yoke of slavery."
- 2 Corinthians 3:17 (ESV) "Now the Lord is a Spirit, and where the Spirit of the Lord is, there is Freedom."
- John 8:32 (ESV) "And you will know the truth, and the truth will set you free."

God Invites, He Doesn't Manipulate

- Matthew 11:28-30 (ESV) "Come to me, all who labor and are heavy laden, and I will give you rest. Take my yoke upon you, and learn from me, for I am gentle and lowly in heart, and you will find rest for your souls. For my yoke is easy, and my burden is light."
- Revelation 3:20 (ESV) "Behold, I stand at the door and knock. If anyone hears my voice and opens the door, I will come in to him and eat with him, and he with me."

God's Perfect Love Casts Out Fear

- 1 John 4;18 (ESV) "There is no fear in love, but perfect love cast out fear. For fear has to do with punishment, and whoever fears has not been perfected in love."
- 2 Timothy 1:7 (ESV) "For God gave us a spirit not of fear but of power and love and self-control."
- Psalm 34:4 (ESV) "I sought the Lord, and he answered me and delivered me from all my fears."
- Isaiah 41:10 (ESV) "Fear not, for I am with you; be not dismayed, for I am your God; I will strengthen you, I will help you, I will uphold you with my righteous right hand."

God Values Us Unconditionally

- Romans 8:38-39 (ESV) "For I am sure that neither death nor life, nor angels nor rulers, nor things present not things to come, nor powers, nor height nor depth, not anything else in all creation, will be able to separate us from the love of God in Christ Jesus our Lord."

- Ephesians 2:4-5 (ESV) "But God, being rich in mercy, because of the great love with which he loved us, even when we were dead in our trespasses, made us alive together with Christ—by grace you have been saved."

God is Gentle and Humble

- Isaiah 42:3 (ESV) "A bruised reed he will not break, and a faintly burning wick he will not quench; he will faithfully bring forth justice."

- Psalms 103:8-10 "The Lord is merciful and gracious, slow to anger and abounding in steadfast love. He will not always chide, nor will he keep his anger forever. He does not deal with us according to our sins, nor repay us according to our iniquities."

God's love Never Controls, manipulates, or abuses.

You are precious to Him. Your voice Matters. Your healing matters.

"With God all things are possible." – Matthew 19:26 (ESV)

Goodwin

BIBLIOGRAPHY

- Bachem, Rachel, Yafet Levin, Gadi Zerach, Maryléne Cloitre, and Zahava Solomon. "The Interpersonal Implications of PTSD and Complex PTSD: The Role of Disturbances in Self-Organization." *Journal of Affective Disorders* 290 (2021): 149-156. https://doi.org/10.1016/j.jad.2021.04.075.

- Bannister, Roger. *The First Four Minutes*. London: Hodder & Stoughton, 1955

- Baylor University School of Social Work. "Adult Clergy Sexual Misconduct: A Study of Understanding, Prevention, and Response." Waco, TX: Baylor University, 2018.Accessed October 29, 2025. https://www.baylor.edu/clergysexualmisconduct/

- Bethune-Cookman University. "Cult Related Activity." Accessed October 29, 2025. https://www.cookman.edu/crt/cult-related-activity.html

- Biali Haas, Susan. The Resilient Life: Manage Stress, Prevent Burnout, and Strengthen Your Mental and Physical Health. Vancouver, BC: Self-published, 2025. https://susanbiali.com/the-resilient-life-book

- Biali Haas, Susan. "Journaling About Trauma and Stress Can Heal Your Body." Psychology Today, December 7, 2019. https://www.psychologytoday.com/us/blog/ prescriptions-life/201912/journaling-about-trauma-and-stress-can-heal-your-body.

- Blue, Ken. Healing Spiritual Abuse: How to Break Free from Bad Church Experiences. Downers Grove, IL: Inter Varsity Press, 1993

- Bouchard, Nicole. "Understanding Trauma: The Healing Process of Poetry." *Tufts Poetry Awards*, March 5, 2019. https://arts.cgu.edu/tufts-poetry-awards/understanding-trauma- the-healing-process-of-poetry/.

- Carmona, Hillary. "The Five Stages of PTSD: Understanding the Process of Healing." *ChoosingTherapy.com.* April 30, 2024. https://www.choosingtherapy.com/stages-of-ptsd/.

- Chaves, Mark, and Diana R. Garland. "The Prevalance of Clergy Sexual Advances Toward Adults in Their Congregations." *Journal for the Scientific Study of Religion* 48, no. 4 (2009): 817-824. Accessed October 29, 2025. https://doi.org/10.1111/j.1468-5906.2009.01472.x.

- Choosing Therapy. "How to Help Someone With PTSD: 14 Tips From a Therapist." Choosing Therapy, April 19, 2024. https://www.choosingtherapy.com/how-to-help-someone-with-ptsd/

- Calhoun, Lawrence G., and Richard G. Tedeschi. Posttraumatic Growth in Clinical Practice. New York: Routledge, 2014

- Clergy Sexual Misconduct Information & Resources. "Adult Clergy Misconduct (CSM) Explained." *ClergySexualMisconduct.com*. Accessed October 29, 2025. https://www.clergysexualmisconduct.com/what-is-csm%3F

- Clergy Sexual Misconduct Information & Resources. "About CSM." Accessed October 30, 2025. https://clergysexualmisconduct.com/

- Cloitre, Marylene, Donn W. Garvert, Julian D. Brewin, Chris R. Bryant, and Richard A. Maercker. "The ISTSS Expert Consensus on Complex PTSD in Adults." *Journal of Traumatic Stress* 26, no. 6 (2013): 610-617. https://doi.org/10.1002/jts.21891

- Cohen, Judith A., and Serene R. Chen. "Trauma-Focused Cognitive Behavioral Therapy for Children and Families." *Child and Adolescent Psychiatric Clinics of North America* 22, no. 2 (2013): 345-361. https://doi.org/10.106/j.chc.2013.01.005.

- Courtois, Christine A., and Julian D. Ford. *Treatment of Complex Trauma: A Sequenced, Relationship-Based Approach.* New York: Guilford Press, 2013

- Cuncic, Arlin. "What is Complex PTSD (C-PTSD)?" *Verywell Mind.* Updated June 27, 2023. https://www.verywellmind.com/what-is-complex-ptsd-5189580.

- Demuth, Mary "A Prayer for Sexual Abuse Victims," *MaryDeMuth.com*, September 23, 2013. Accessed October 29, 2025. https://www.marydemuth.com/a-prayer-for-sexual-abuse-victims/

- Doehring, Carrie. "Military Moral Injury: An Evidence-Based and Intercultural Approach to Spiritual Care." Pastoral Psychology 68, no. 1 (2019): 15-30. https://doi.org/10.1007/ s11089-018-0813-5

- Drossman, Douglas A., E. Lesserman, V. Li, M. Gluck, D. Toomey, and N. Mitchell. "Sexual and Physical Abuse and Gastrointestinal Illness: Review and Recommendations." *Annals of Internal Medicine* 123, no. 10 (November 15, 1995): 782-794, https://doi.org/10.7326/0003-4819-123-10-199511150-00002.

- Elliot, Deborah M., Kevin D. Browne, and Jennifer Kilcoyne. "Child Sexual Abuse: A Study of Female Victims' Perspectives." *Child Abuse & Neglect* 19, no 5. (1995): 579-588. Accessed October 29, 2025. https://doi.org/10.1016/0145-2134(95)00033-O.

- Enright, Robert D., and Richard P. Fitzgibbons. Helping Clients Forgive: An Empirical Guide for Resolving Anger and Restoring Hope. 2nd ed. Washington, DC: American Psychological Association, 2015.

- Enroth, Ronald M. *Churches That Abuse.* Grand Rapids, MI: Zondervan, 1992.

- Felitti, Vincent J., Robert F. Anda, Dale Nordenberg, David F. Williamson, Alison M. Spitz, Valerie Edwards, Mary P. Koss, and James S. Marks. "Relationship of Childhood Abuse and Household

Dysfunction to Many of the Leading Causes of Death in Adults: The Adverse Childhood Experiences (ACE) Study." *American Journal of Preventative Medicine* 14, no. 4 (May 1998): 245-258. https://doi.org/10.1016/S0749-3797(98)00017-8.

- Fortune, Marie M., and James Newton Poling. Sexual Abuse by Clergy: A Crisis for the Church. Eugene, OR: Wipf and Stock Publishers, 2020.

- Freedman, Suzanne, and Robert D. Enright. Forgiveness Education: A Pathway to Emotional Healing and Education for Children and Adults. Springfield, IL: Charles C. Thomas, 2015

- Garland, Diana R., and Christy Argueta. How Clergy Sexual Misconduct Happens: A Qualitative Study of First-Person Accounts. Waco, TX: Baylor University, Diana R. Garland School of Social Work, 2010. https://www.baylor.edu/ssw/index.php?id=869704.

- Garland, Diana R., and Christy Argueta. How Clergy Sexual Misconduct Happens: A Qualitative Study of First-Person Accounts. Waco, TX: Diana R. Garland School of Social Work, Baylor University, 2010. https://www.baylor.edu/content/services/document.php/96038.pdf.

- Gold, Richard. *Writing with At-Risk Youth: The Pongo Teen Writing Method.* Lanham, MD: Rowman & Littlefield Education, 2014.

- HealthMatch. "A Guide to the Stages of Complex PTSD Recovery." *HealthMatch*, September 20, 2022. https://healthmatch.io/ptsd/complex-ptsd-recovery-stages.

- Herman, Judith Lewis. *Trauma and Recovery: The Aftermath of Violence—From Domestic Abuse to Political Terror.* New York: Basic Books, 1992

- Hoffman, Louis. Letters for My Father: Grief, Love, and Self-Exploration. Colorado Springs, CO: University Professors Press, 2023. https://

universityprofessorspress.com/louis-hoffman-phd-upp-author.

- Hopkins, Rebecca. "Some Churches Call Clergy Sexual Misconduct an 'Affair.' Survivors Are Fighting to Make It Against the Law." *Christianity Today*, August 17, 2023. https://www.christianitytoday.com/news/2023/august/church-clergy-sexual-misconduct-assault-consent-pooler.html.

- Johnson, David, and Jeff VanVonderen. The Subtle Power of Spiritual Abuse: Recognizing and Escaping Spiritual Manipulation and False Spiritual Authority Within the Church. Minneapolis: Bethany House Publishers, 1991

- Karatzias, Eirini, Marylene Cloitre, Chris R. Bryant, Andreas Maercker, et al. "Complex Posttraumatic Stress Disorder in DSM-5 and ICD-11: Clinical and Diagnostic Implications." European Journal of Psychotraumatology 8, no. 1 (2017): 1340835. https://doi.org/10.1080/20008198.2017.1340835.

- King-White, Dakota. "Post-Traumatic Stress Disorder: Symptoms, Causes, & Treatment." *ChoosingTherapy.com.* Reviewed by Benjamin Troy MD. Published June 6, 2022. https://www.choosingtherapy.com/ptsd/.

- Krause-Utz, Annett, Simone E. Winter, Babette Renneberg, and Christian Schmahl. "Neurobiological Correlates of Complex Posttraumatic Stress Disorder and Borderline Personality Disorder: A Systematic Review." *Borderline Personality Disorder and Emotion Dysregulation* 4 (2017): 11. https://doi.org/10.1186/s40479-017-0066-6.

- Langberg, Diane, 2016. "Helping the Traumatized." *CareLeader*, September 20. https://careleader.org/shepherding-the-traumatized/

- Langberg, Diane. *"Suffering and the Heart of God: How Trauma Destroys and Christ Restores."* Greensboro, NC: New Growth Press, 2015.

- Lanius, Ruth., Eric Vermetten, Richard J. Loewenstein, Bethany Brand, Christian Schmahl, J. Douglas Bremner and David Spiegel. "Emotion Modulation in PTSD: Clinical and Neurobiological Evidence for a Dissociative Subtype." American Journal of Psychiatry 167, no. 6 (June 2010): 640-647. https://doi.org/10.1176/appi.ajp.2009.09081168.

- Levine, Peter A. *Waking the Tiger*: Healing Trauma. Berkeley, CA: North Atlantic Books, 1997.

- Lieberman, Allison. "Healing Sexual Trauma: 6 Tips from a Therapist." Choosing Therapy, accessed October 29, 2025. https://www.choosingtherapy.com/sexual-trauma-healing/.

- Mackenzie, Ian K. 2004. "The Stockholm Syndrome Revisited: Hostages, Relationships, Prediction, Control and Psychological Science." "Journal of Police Crisis Negotiations." 4, no. 1 (February): 5-21 https://doi.org/10.1300/J173v04n01_02

- Masten, Ann S. "Ordinary Magic: Resilience Processes in Development." *American Psychologist* 56, no. 3 (2001): 227–238.

- McEwen, Bruce S. "The End of Stress as We Know It." Washington, DC: Joseph Henry Press, 2017.

- McEwen, Bruce S. "Neurobiological and Systemic Effects of Chronic Stress." *Chronic Stress* 1 (2017): 1-11. https://doi.org/10.1177/2470547017692328.

- McMackin, Robert A., Joseph M. Keane, and Elspeth Cameron Ritchie, eds. Trauma, Recovery, and Growth: Positive Psychological Perspectives on Posttraumatic Stress. Hoboken, NJ: Wiley, 2017.

- Merriam-Webster. "Debauchery." *Merriam-Webster. com Dictionary*. Accessed October 29, 2025. https://www.merriam-webster.com/dictionary/debauchery.

- NetGrace. "Certification: Safeguarding the Church." NetGrace. Accessed October 30, 2025. https://netgrace.org/certification.

- Oakley, Lisa Ruth, and Kathryn Susan Kinmond. Breaking the Silence on Spiritual Abuse. Basingstoke: Palgrave Macmillan, 2013.

- Panahi, Naghmeh. "Consensual Relationships Don't Result in Trauma and Lifelong Suffering." Christianity Today, December 5, 2022. https://www.christianitytoday.com

- Paras, Melissa L., Jordan B. Murad, W. John Chen, Kirstin A. Goranson, Nicole J. Sattler, Beth R. Colbenson, et al. "Sexual Abuse and Lifetime Diagnosis of Somatic Disorders: A Systematic Review and Meta-analysis." *JAMA* 302, no 5 (2009) 550-561. https://doi.org/10.1001.jama.2009.1091.

- Pargament, Kenneth I. Spiritually Integrated Psychotherapy: Understanding and Addressing the Sacred. 2nd ed. New York: Guilford Press, 2021

- Pargament, Kenneth I., Julie J. Exline, and James W. Jones, eds. APA Handbook of Psychology, Religion, and Spirituality. Vol. 1. Washington, DC: American Psychological Association, 2013.

- Pellauer, David. Sexual Assault and Abuse. Edited by M. M. Fortune and J. Hertze. London: Sage Publications, 2018.

- Pellauer, Mary D., Barbara Chester, and Jane Boyajian, eds. Sexual Assault and Abuse: A Handbook for Clergy and Religious Professionals. San Francisco: Harper & Row, 1987

- Pennebaker, James W., and Sandra K. Beall. "Confronting a Traumatic Event: Toward an

Understanding of Inhibition and Disease." *Journal of Abnormal Psychology* 95, no. 3 (1986): 274-281. https://doi.org/10.1037/0021-843X.95.3.274.

- Pooler, David K., and Liza Barros-Lane. "A National Study of Adult Women Sexually Abused by Clergy: Insights for Social Workers." Social Work 67, no. 2 (2022): 123-133. https://doi.org/10.1093/sw/swac001.

- Porges, Stephen W. "Polyvagal Theory: A Science of Safety." *Frontiers in Integrative Neuroscience* 16 (May 2022): 1-9. Accessed October 29, 2025. https://doi.org/10.3389/fnint.2022.871227.

- PTSD UK. "Running Can Help Reduce PTSD Symptoms." *Facebook,* August 21, 2019. https://www.ptsduk.org/running-can-help-reduce-ptsd-symptoms/.

- PTSD UK. "The Science Behind Music Therapy." *PTSD UK,* accessed October 30, 2025. https://www.ptsduk.org/the-science-behind-music-therapy/.

- PTSD UK. "How Progressive Muscle Relaxation Can Help People with PTSD." *PTSD UK.* Accessed October 30, 2025. https://www.ptsduk.org/progressive-muscle-relaxation/.

- Rooney, Mariah. "The Healing Power of Strength Training." The New York Times, March 5, 2021. https:// www.nytimes.com/2021/03/05/well/move/strength-training-mental-health.html.

- Royal Commission into Institutional Responses to Child Sexual Abuse. *Final Report, Volume 16: Religious Institutions.* Canberra: Commonwealth of Australia, 2017 Accessed October 29, 2025. https://www.childabuseroyalcommission.gov.au/religious-institutions

- Rudolfsson, Lisa, and Inga Tidefors. 'Shepherd My Sheep': Clerical Readiness to Meet Psychological and Existential Needs from Victims of Sexual Abuse."

Pastoral Psychology 58, no. 1 (2009): 79-92. https://doi.org/10.1007/ s11089-008-0183-7

- Rudolfsson, Gudrun, and Inga Tidefors. "The Process of Spiritual Healing after Sexual Abuse by Clergy: Narrative Analysis of Survivors' Stories." The International Journal for the   Psychology of Religion 25, no. 3 (2015): 201-218. https://doi.org/ 10.1080/10508619.2014.918779

- Smith, Marquette J. The 7 Steps of Spiritual Abuse. Self-published, 1991

- Substance Abuse and Mental Health Services Administration (SAMHSA). *SAMHSA's Concept of Trauma and Guidance for a Trauma-Informed Approach.* HHS Publication No. (SMA) 14-4884. Rockville, MD: Substance Abuse and Mental Health Services Administration, 2014. https://ncsacw.acf.hhs.gov/ userfiles/files/SAMHSA_trauma.pdf.

- Ullman, Sarah E., and Liana Peter-Hagene. "Social Reactions to Sexual Assault Disclosure, Coping, Perceived Control, and PTSD Symptoms in Sexual Assault Victims." *Journal of Community Psychology* 42, no. 4 (2014): 495-508. https://doi.org/10.1002/ jcop.21624

- U.S. Department of Veterans Affairs, National Center for PTSD. Factors That Influence Recovery from PTSD. Washington, DC: U.S. Department of Veterans Affairs, 2024. https:// www.ptsd.va.gov.

- University of Texas at Austin. "UT Researchers: Running May Help Treat PTSD. *The Alcalde*, July 7, 2015. https://alcalde.texasexes.org/2015/07/ut-researchers-running-may-help-treat-ptsd/.

- Van der Kolk, Bessel A. *The Body Keeps the Score: Brain, Mind, and Body in the Healing of Trauma*, New York: Viking, 2014

- Wade, Nathaniel G., Everett L. Worthington Jr., Don E. Meyer, and Julie A. Bauman. "Promoting

Forgiveness: A Meta-Analysis of Psychological Interventions." *Journal of Counseling Psychology* 61, no. 2 (2014): 166–176.

- Wong, Serena. "Putting the Pieces Together with Kenneth Pargament." Spirituality in Clinical Practice 9, no. 1 (2022): 1-6. https://doi.org/10.1037/scp0000266

- World Health Organization. *International Classification of Diseases, 11th Revision (ICD-11) Complex Post Traumatic Stress Disorder (6B41)*. Geneva: World Health Organization, 2018. https://icd.who.int.

- Worthington, Everett L., Jr., and Diane Langberg. *Forgiving and Reconciling: Bridges to Wholeness and Hope*. Downers Grove, IL: InterVarsity Press, 2012.

Scripture References/Sources

- Crossway Bibles. *The Holy Bible: English Standard Version*. Wheaton, IL: Crossway Bibles, 2001. Referenced verses: Genesis 18:25; Joshua 7:1; Matthew 5:7; Matthew 6:14–15; Matthew 7:9–11; Matthew 10:40–42; Matthew 18:21–22; Matthew 19:26; Psalms 16:8; Psalms 23:6; Psalms 27:13; Psalms 34:8; Psalms 91:1–2; John 8:31; Romans 12:2; Romans 15:4; 2 Corinthians 12:7–9; Colossians 1:17–18; Luke 23:43; 1 Corinthians 6:19–20. Data derived from a word concordance search of the word "forgiveness and forgive" in the ESV.

- Cruden, Alexander. *Cruden's Complete Concordance to the Holy Scriptures*. Revised and reprinted. Peabody, MA: Hendrickson Publishers, 1992 — confirms that all forms of the word "forgive" (including forgive, forgiven, forgiveth, forgiving, and forgiveness) occur approximately 126 times in the King James Version, and that "forgive" appears approximately 23 times in the New Testament.

- Peterson, Eugene H. *The Message: The Bible in Contemporary Language*. Colorado Springs, CO: NavPress, 2002. Referenced verse: 1 Corinthians 11:13–16.

- The Holy Bible: *King James Version. Cambridge Edition*, 1769; reprint, Peabody, MA: Hendrickson Publishers, 2004. Referenced verses: 1 Samuel 17:29; 1 Peter 4:17; Titus 3:10; Joshua 7:1; Genesis 18:25.

About the Author

Bridget Goodwin is a missionary, musician, minister of music, podcaster, writer, and worship leader on YouTube.

In 2015, while living in the UK, she and her husband founded Harvest Labourers International to connect people worldwide with Jesus Christ. After moving back to the US in 2017, Bridget began her journey of healing from sexual abuse from her youth. After keeping this secret for 40 years, she found healing as she discovered her voice through counseling and therapy. She is now an advocate for sexual trauma victims.

Her ministry, "I Have a Voice," hosts summits, conferences, and workshops for those who have suffered sexual and religious trauma.

Bridget's mission is for women and men to find their voice, step out in bravery, and embrace the transformative power of hope found in Jesus.

When she's not ministering or teaching, Bridget enjoys running marathons and spending time in nature with her Golden Retriever, Lady Elle. She teaches piano, voice, and instruments privately, primarily traveling to students' homes as an itinerant teacher.

About I Have A Voice Ministries

"I have a voice, we have a voice."

I Have A Voice Ministries was founded to give survivors of sexual abuse safe spaces to share their stories and break their silence.

An abuser takes your voice away and silences you. Our mission is to help you get it back. Your voice is one of many—whether weak or strong, it is your key to deliverance.

What We Offer

- Healing Workshops & Retreats
- Safe spaces where survivors can share without fear or judgment.
- Healing Circles
- Gatherings led with licensed therapists and counselors who understand trauma's unique challenges.
- Community Building
- A place where you belong, where you don't need to hide, where your hurt and shame are understood because we've been there too.

Five-Step Healing Framework

1. Breaking the Silence
2. Recognizing the Patterns
3. Reclaiming Your Identity
4. Building Your Community
5. Finding Your Purpose

Resources & Support

Tools to help you reclaim yourself daily, and support for loved ones who want to help survivors on their healing journey.

Our Belief

Through the blood of Jesus, we will give you purpose and hope. You will know that you are not alone. We will walk alongside you as you step out in bravery.

Whether you are a survivor or someone who wants to help a loved one or friend, we are here to equip you with resources and tools.

We must stand together and stop sexual abuse.

Our Symbol

An open cage with a bird set to flight—representing freedom from silence.

Connect With Us

Website: www.ihaveavoice.love

Join us for healing workshops, worship gatherings, and community support.

"And you will know the truth, and the truth will set you free."
— John 8:32 (ESV)

You are not alone. Your voice matters.

Your story deserves to be told.

We have a voice.